Strength Band Training

SECOND EDITION

Phil Page
PhD, PT, ATC, CSCS

Todd Ellenbecker
DPT, MS, SCS, OCS, CSCS

Human Kinetics

Library of Congress Cataloging-in-Publication Data

Page, Phillip, 1967-
  Strength band training / Phil Page, Todd Ellenbecker. -- 2nd ed.
    p. cm.
  ISBN-13: 978-0-7360-9037-7 (softcover)
  ISBN-10: 0-7360-9037-1 (softcover)
  1. Isometric exercise. I. Ellenbecker, Todd S., 1962- II. Title.
  RA781.2.P34 2011
  613.7'149--dc22

                                    2010030751

ISBN-10: 0-7360-9037-1 (print)
ISBN-13: 978-0-7360-9037-7 (print)

Copyright © 2011 by Benchmark PT and Todd Ellenbecker
Copyright © 2005 by Phil Page and Todd Ellenbecker

This publication is written and published to provide accurate and authoritative information relevant to the subject matter presented. It is published and sold with the understanding that the author and publisher are not engaged in rendering legal, medical, or other professional services by reason of their authorship or publication of this work. If medical or other expert assistance is required, the services of a competent professional person should be sought.

Acquisitions Editor: Justin Klug; **Developmental Editor:** Carla Zych; **Assistant Editors:** Michael Bishop, Elizabeth Evans, and Steven Calderwood; **Copyeditor:** Mary Rivers; **Permission Manager:** Martha Gullo; **Graphic Designer:** Nancy Rasmus; **Graphic Artist:** Julie L. Denzer; **Cover Designer:** Keith Blomberg; **Photographer:** Neil Bernstein; **Photo Asset Manager:** Laura Fitch; **Visual Production Assistant:** Joyce Brumfield; **Photo Production Manager:** Jason Allen; **Art Manager:** Kelly Hendren; **Associate Art Manager:** Alan L. Wilborn; **Medical Illustrations:** © Human Kinetics; **Printer:** Sheridan Books

Human Kinetics books are available at special discounts for bulk purchase. Special editions or book excerpts can also be created to specification. For details, contact the Special Sales Manager at Human Kinetics.

Printed in the United States of America   10 9 8 7 6 5 4 3 2 1

The paper in this book is certified under a sustainable forestry program.

Human Kinetics
Web site: www.HumanKinetics.com

United States: Human Kinetics
P.O. Box 5076
Champaign, IL 61825-5076
800-747-4457
e-mail: humank@hkusa.com

Canada: Human Kinetics
475 Devonshire Road Unit 100
Windsor, ON N8Y 2L5
800-465-7301 (in Canada only)
e-mail: info@hkcanada.com

Europe: Human Kinetics
107 Bradford Road
Stanningley
Leeds LS28 6AT, United Kingdom
+44 (0) 113 255 5665
e-mail: hk@hkeurope.com

Australia: Human Kinetics
57A Price Avenue
Lower Mitcham, South Australia 5062
08 8372 0999
e-mail: info@hkaustralia.com

New Zealand: Human Kinetics
P.O. Box 80
Torrens Park, South Australia 5062
0800 222 062
e-mail: info@hknewzealand.com

E5065

To my family—Angela, Madison, Caitlin, Hannah, and Andrew—for their patience, understanding, and encouragement.

—Phil Page

To Gail, for her love and support.

—Todd Ellenbecker

CONTENTS

EXERCISE FINDER

Title	Primary muscles affected	Primary sport applications	Attachment required	Page number
CHAPTER 3				
Lateral raise	Deltoids	Basketball, football, hockey	No	32
Front raise	Deltoids	Basketball, football, hockey	No	33
Scaption	Rotator cuff, deltoids	All sports	No	34
Shoulder internal rotation at 0 degrees	Rotator cuff	Baseball, golf, softball, swimming, tennis, volleyball	Yes	35
Shoulder external rotation at 0 degrees	Rotator cuff	Baseball, golf, softball, swimming, tennis, volleyball	Yes	36
Serratus punch	Serratus anterior	Baseball, golf, softball, swimming, tennis, volleyball	Yes	37
Biceps curl	Biceps	All sports	No	38
Elbow extension	Triceps	All sports	Yes	39
Wrist flexion	Wrist flexors	Baseball, golf, softball, tennis, volleyball	No	40
Wrist extension	Wrist extensors	Baseball, golf, softball, tennis, volleyball	No	41
Forearm supination	Supinator, biceps	Baseball, golf, softball, tennis, volleyball	No	42
Forearm pronation	Pronator teres	Baseball, golf, softball, tennis, volleyball	No	43
Ulnar deviation	Forearm flexors and extensors	Baseball, golf, softball, tennis, volleyball	No	44
Radial deviation	Forearm flexors and extensors	Baseball, golf, softball, tennis, volleyball	No	45
Hip internal rotation	Hip rotators	All sports	Yes	46
Hip external rotation	Hip rotators	All sports	Yes	47
Hip flexion	Iliopsoas	All sports	Yes	48
Hip extension	Gluteus maximus	All sports	Yes	49
Hip abduction	Gluteus medius	All sports	Yes	50
Hip adduction	Hip adductors	All sports	Yes	51
Knee flexion	Hamstrings	All sports	Yes	52
Knee extension	Quadriceps	All sports	Yes	53
Terminal knee extension	Quadriceps, vastus medialis	All sports	Yes	54
Dorsiflexion	Tibialis anterior	All sports	No	55
Plantar flexion	Gastrocnemius and soleus	All sports	No	56
Inversion	Tibialis posterior	All sports	No	57
Eversion	Peroneals	All sports	No	58

> *continued*

Title	Primary muscles affected	Primary sport applications	Attachment required	Page number
Shoulder wall walk	Rotator cuff, lower trapezius	Baseball, softball, swimming, tennis, volleyball	No	82
Shoulder monster walk	Serratus anterior	Baseball, softball, swimming, tennis, volleyball	No	83
CHAPTER 5				
Abdominal crunch	Abdominals	All sports	Yes	86
Oblique curl-up	Oblique abdominals	All sports	Yes	87
Lower abdominal crunch	Lower abdominals	All sports	No	88
Kneeling crunch	Abdominals	All sports	Yes	89
Trunk rotation	Oblique abdominals	All sports	No	90
Side bend	Quadratus lumborum	All sports	No	91
Seated back extension	Multifidus	All sports	No	92
Standing back extension	Back extensors, gluteus maximus	All sports	No	93
Side bridge	Quadratus lumborum	All sports	No	94
Quadruped stabilization	Lumbar stabilizers	All sports	No	95
Supine stabilization	Lumbar stabilizers	All sports	No	96
CHAPTER 6				
Hip lift	Iliopsoas	Basketball, football, hockey, soccer	No	99
Bridge	Gluteus maximus	Basketball, football, hockey, soccer	No	100
Unilateral bridge	Gluteus maximus	Basketball, football, hockey, soccer	No	101
Hip extension (donkey kick)	Gluteus maximus	Basketball, football, hockey, soccer	No	102
Side-lying hip lift	Gluteus medius	All sports	No	103
Clam	Hip rotators	All sports	No	104
Reverse clam	Hip rotators	All sports	No	105
Good morning	Gluteus maximus, hamstrings	Basketball, football, hockey, soccer	No	106
Closed-chain hip rotation	Hip rotators, gluteus maximus, ankle stabilizers	All sports	No	107
Lunge	Gluteus maximus, quadriceps	All sports	No	108

Title	Primary muscles affected	Primary sport applications	Attach-ment required	Page number
Lateral lunge	Gluteus medius, gluteus maximus, quadriceps	All sports	No	109
Squat	Gluteus maximus, quadriceps	All sports	No	110
Barbell squat	Gluteus maximus, quadriceps	Basketball, football, hockey, soccer	No	111
Single-leg squat	Gluteus maximus, quadriceps, ankle stabilizers	All sports	No	112
Monster walk	Gluteus medius, gluteus maximus, quadriceps	All sports	No	113
Squat walk	Gluteus maximus, gluteus medius, quadriceps	All sports	No	114
Leg press	Gluteus maximus, quadriceps	All sports	No	115
Standing leg pull-through	Hamstrings, gluteus maximus	Basketball, football, hockey, soccer	Yes	116
Thera-Band kick	Gluteus maximus, gluteus medius, iliopsoas, quadri-ceps, ankle stabi-lizers	All sports	Yes	117
CHAPTER 7				
Squat with diagonal flexion	Deltoids, lumbar stabilizers, quadriceps	All sports	No	120
Lunge with diagonal flexion	Deltoids, lumbar stabilizers, quadriceps	All sports	No	121
Bilateral chop	Anterior trunk, shoulder	Basketball, football, hockey	Yes	122
Bilateral lift	Posterior trunk, shoulder	Basketball, football, hockey	Yes	123
Unilateral row with side bridge	Rhomboids, qua-dratus lumborum	Baseball, softball, swim-ming, tennis, volleyball	Yes	124
Step push	Pectoralis major, triceps	Basketball, football, hockey	No	125
Lift simulation	Gluteus maximus, quadriceps, lumbar stabilizers	Basketball, football, hockey	No	126
Step lift	Gluteus maximus, quadriceps, lumbar stabilizers	Basketball, football, hockey	No	127

> continued

Title	Primary muscles affected	Primary sport applications	Attachment required	Page number
Step incline press	Pectoralis major, triceps, deltoids	Basketball, football, hockey	No	128
Reverse step pull	Rhomboids, latissimus dorsi	Basketball, football, hockey	Yes	129
Step-up	Quadriceps, gluteus maximus, biceps	Baseball, golf, softball, swimming, tennis, volleyball	No	130
Shoulder external rotation step	Rotator cuff, rhomboids, trunk rotators	Baseball, golf, softball, swimming, tennis, volleyball	Yes	131
Shoulder internal rotation step	Rotator cuff, pectoralis major, trunk rotators	Baseball, golf, softball, swimming, tennis, volleyball	Yes	132
CHAPTER 8				
Resisted running	Lower extremity muscle groups	Running, football, soccer, baseball, softball	Yes	134
Resisted backward running	Lower extremity muscle groups	Football, soccer, baseball, softball	Yes	135
Acceleration	Lower extremity muscle groups	Running, football, soccer, baseball, softball	Yes	136
Assisted sprinting	Quadriceps, gastrocnemius, soleus	Running, football, soccer, baseball, softball	Yes	137
Reciprocal arm and leg action	Hip flexors, quadriceps, core stabilizers	Running, football, soccer, baseball, softball	Yes	138
Overhead throw	Core muscles, subscapularis, pectoralis major, latissimus dorsi	Baseball, softball, football	Yes	139
Underhand throw	Anterior deltoid, pectoralis major, hip extensors, quadriceps, wrist flexors, gastrocnemius	Softball	Yes	140
Bilateral overhead throw	Core muscles, latissimus dorsi, triceps	Basketball, soccer	Yes	141
Arm acceleration drill	Rotator cuff, scapular stabilizers	Baseball, softball, football	Yes	142
Plyometric shoulder external rotation 90/90	Rotator cuff, scapular stabilizers	Baseball, softball, football	Yes	143

Title	Primary muscles affected	Primary sport applications	Attachment required	Page number
Biceps plyometric elbow extension	Biceps, brachialis, brachioradialis, anterior deltoid	Baseball, softball, football	Yes	144
Kick simulation	Lower extremity muscle groups, core muscles	Soccer, football	Yes	145
Hamstring plyometric hip flexion	Hamstrings, gluteus maximus, gluteus medius	Soccer, football	Yes	146
Quick kick	Core muscles, gluteus medius	Soccer, football	No	147
Bat swing simulation	All muscle groups	Baseball, softball	Yes	148
Tennis forehand	All muscle groups	Tennis	Yes	149
Tennis backhand	Posterior deltoid, rotator cuff, scapular stabilizers, core muscles	Tennis	Yes	150
Elbow extension with shoulder elevation	Triceps, core muscles	Tennis	No	151
Golf swing	Upper extremity muscle groups, core muscles	Golf	Yes	152
Swim pull-through	Latissimus dorsi, triceps, core muscles	Swimming	Yes	153
Jump	Lower extremity muscle groups, core muscles	Soccer, basketball, volleyball	Yes	154
Hop landing	Quadriceps, hip extensors, gluteus medius, core muscles	Soccer, basketball, volleyball	No	155
Jump down	Quadriceps, hip extensors, gluteus medius, core muscles	Soccer, basketball, volleyball	No	156
Side jump	Lower extremity muscle groups, core muscles	Soccer, basketball, volleyball	Yes	157
Resisted plyometric lateral jump step	Quadriceps, hip extensors, gastrocnemius, core muscles	Soccer, basketball, volleyball	Yes	158

> *continued*

ACKNOWLEDGMENTS

Thanks to the Hygenic Corporation, makers of Thera-Band, for their support of research and education with elastic resistance.

Thanks to our friends, colleagues, patients, students, and readers, who continue to teach us every day.

Strength training is an important component of any well-rounded exercise program. In fact, the American College of Sports Medicine and the U.S. Department of Health and Human Services recommend that muscle strengthening exercises be performed at least two days a week, using all major muscle groups. Elastic resistance bands offer an inexpensive, convenient, and effective way of adding resistance exercises to any workout. Research has proven the effectiveness of elastic resistance training (ERT) across ages, from children to older adults, as well as from sedentary people to elite athletes.

Elastic resistance has been used for over 100 years in fitness programs, and more recently, in rehabilitation. It's one of the most-used modes of resistance training by physical therapists for both clinical and home programs. Because of its versatility, elastic resistance is ideal for a variety of patients and conditions. Recent research has shown that elastic resistance provides results similar to those of traditional isotonic resistance, making it ideal for anyone to use.

This second edition of *Strength Band Training* has been improved with new photos, more exercises, and sections on performance enhancement. Part I includes a chapter covering the basics of elastic resistance training, such as force production and general use of the bands. Stretching exercises using elastic resistance (chapter 2) are also introduced.

Part II introduces the use of elastic resistance bands for stability, strength, and power. It includes six chapters full of exercises, beginning with isolated joint exercises (chapter 3). These exercises can be used for single joint movements in fitness or rehabilitation. Regional, multijoint exercises are then provided for the upper body, core, and lower body (chapters 4-6). Part II concludes with total body exercises, including more functional movements (chapter 7), as well as exercises for power, speed, and agility (chapter 8).

A major advantage and application of elastic resistance training is the ability to perform virtually any training movement and to perform that movement in various places and situations. This makes ERT an ideal method of training for those with fitness, rehabilitation, and sport-specific exercise needs. Part III offers sample program options for fitness and sport applications.

The programs in chapter 9 can be used under normal circumstances as well as when time is limited or when access to standard workout equipment is difficult or impossible. Long (30-minute) and short (15-minute) versions of highly efficient ERT circuit programs for each of the three major regions of the body—the upper body, core, and lower body—are presented. These can be performed alone or in whatever combination best suits individual goals and circumstances.

ERT programs tailored to the sport athletes take part in can be found in chapters 10 (rotational sports), 11 (strength and power sports), and 12 (endurance sports). The programs use base exercises and sport simulation exercises that will enhance performance while preventing or minimizing injuries.

Base exercises are recommended for athletes for two primary reasons: to activate or develop muscles that are used repetitively or at very high levels by athletes in that sport, and to achieve muscle balance by working muscles that are underdeveloped as a result of sport-specific adaptations. Lunge exercises, for example, would be appropriate for athletes who jump or push off in an explosive, powerful manner because they work the quadriceps, gluteals, and calf musculature used by athletes during lower body movement. External shoulder rotation exercises would suit rotational sport athletes, not by developing the external rotators that provide power to strike or throw a ball, but by enhancing balance and stability to counteract the adaptation in the more powerful internal rotators brought about by sport participation.

Performing sport simulation movements with the overload provided by elastic resistance serves to develop the primary muscles that are used during sport-specific movement patterns, as well as specifically train the body to do the movements required to achieve success within the sport.

PART I

Basics of Elastic Resistance Training

Strength Training With Elastic Resistance

The secret to elastic resistance exercise is simple. As you stretch the elastic band, the resistance increases. This resistance provides a progressive stimulus to the muscle to build strength and help increase muscle mass. Elastic resistance training (ERT) allows us to exercise single or multiple joints at one time, making exercises more functional and efficient. Regular exercise machines and dumbbells use gravity against the weights (isotonic resistance) and often limit you to one particular exercise per machine. Elastic resistance, on the other hand, doesn't rely on gravity; rather, its resistance depends on how much the band or tubing is stretched.

Many exercises can be performed with a single band or tube, and the resistance can easily be increased by moving to the next higher color of band or tube. The different colors of bands represent increasing thicknesses of the band, which ultimately increase the force. Figure 1.1 shows that moving from one color band to the next increases resistance by 20 to 30 percent when the bands are stretched to twice their resting length.

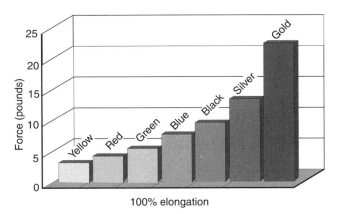

Figure 1.1 Force of Thera-Band elastic bands at 100 percent elongation.

Force Production

The force produced by an elastic band or tube is determined by this formula: force = cross section area × percent elongation. The cross section area is essentially the total amount of elastic material (width × height), while the percent elongation is the percentage of change in length from the resting (no tension) length. For example, a 3-foot length of band with no tension stretched to a final length of 6 feet has elongated 100 percent. Table 1.1 illustrates the force produced at various percentages of elongation.

Table 1.1   Force Production of Thera-Band Elastic Bands

	Yellow	Red	Green	Blue	Black	Silver	Gold
25%	1.1	1.5	2	2.8	3.6	5	7.9
50%	1.8	2.6	3.2	4.6	6.3	8.5	13.9
75%	2.4	3.3	4.2	5.9	8.1	11.1	18.1
100%	2.9	3.9	5	7.1	9.7	13.2	21.6
125%	3.4	4.4	5.7	8.1	11	15.2	24.6
150%	3.9	4.9	6.5	9.1	12.3	17.1	27.5
175%	4.3	5.4	7.2	10.1	13.5	18.9	30.3
200%	4.8	5.9	7.9	11.1	14.8	21	33.4
225%	5.3	6.4	8.8	12.1	16.2	23	36.6
250%	5.8	7	9.6	13.3	17.6	25.3	40.1

Data from P. Page, A. Labbe, and R. Topp, 2000, "Clinical force production at Thera-Band elastic bands," *Journal of Orthopaedic & Sports Physical Therapy* 30(1): A47-48.

One exercise band can be used to strengthen all the major muscle groups with exercises, such as a bench press, seated row, upright row, lat pull-down, leg press, knee extension, or hamstring curl. Elastic bands may also be used to strengthen specific muscles that can't be activated with selectorized (muscle-specific) machines, such as the rotator cuff and peroneus longus (a muscle important to foot pronation). In addition, bands can be used to perform flexibility or balance exercises. Table 1.2 compares elastic and isotonic resistance.

Table 1.2   Comparison of Isotonic and Elastic Resistance

Characteristic	Isotonic machines	Elastic resistance
Resistance source	Gravity and mass	% stretch
Force profile	Linear and constant	Linear and ascending
Strength curve	Bell shaped	Bell shaped
Movement patterns	Fixed	Variable

According to the American College of Sports Medicine (ACSM), strength training is an important part of any well-rounded exercise program for all adults, including older adults. In 2008, the United States Department of Health and Human Services included strength training in national physical activity guidelines, recommending that two or more days a week, adults perform moderate- to high-intensity muscle-strengthening activities of all the major muscle groups.

Research demonstrates that ERT provides as much benefit in strength gains as the use of more expensive and bulky weight-training equipment. A 2008 study by Colado & Triplett compared 10 weeks of elastic- and machine-based exercise at the same intensities (Effects of a short-term resistance program using elastic bands versus weight machines for sedentary middle-aged women. *J Strength Cond Res*. 22(5):1441-1448). The researchers found no significant difference between the groups: both the elastic- and machine-based groups significantly increased their strength and muscle mass. Furthermore, the researchers pointed out that the elastic resistance exercisers benefited from lower cost and less space for training compared to the machine-based exercisers.

Simply performing an exercise program for as little as 6 weeks with elastic resistance can increase strength 10 to 30 percent in both younger and older adults. The added benefits of ERT include increasing muscle mass, lowering body fat, and increasing power and endurance. In fact, strength training of the legs with elastic resistance can even help improve your balance, gait, and mobility. Elastic resistance training provides a variety of training methods. In addition to strength training, elastic resistance is used for retraining movement patterns by creating a vector of resistance during sport-specific activities such as a golf swing or baseball pitch. Elastic resistance can also be used for stabilization training by targeting the core muscles through whole-body exercises.

Elastic bands have also been combined with isotonic resistance for high-performance training, particularly when paired with a bench press or squat movement. Theoretically, combining elastic and isotonic resistances complements both concentric and eccentric movement phases to provide greater acceleration in the initial movement, possibly enhancing power. However, the literature is somewhat conflicting; some studies report improvements in strength and power with combined elastic and isotonic resistance, while others do not. More research is needed to confirm the theory.

Advantages and Disadvantages

As with any mode of strength training, elastic resistance has several advantages and disadvantages. Athletes considering the incorporation of ERT into their training regiment should carefully weigh these issues.

Advantages

The greatest advantages of elastic resistance are its portability, low cost, and versatility. Unlike isotonic resistance (free weights, machines, and pulleys), elastic resistance relies on the tension within the band rather than the pull of gravity. While isotonic resistance exercises are limited to directions of movement in which gravity provides resistance (such as upward movements against gravity), elastic resistance offers many more movements and directions of motion for exercises (such as side-to-side movements). This imparts a higher level of neuromuscular control compared to selectorized machines. Elastic resistance allows us to exercise multiple joints and planes in a standing position (rather than seated on machines), thus bringing more core muscle activation into the same machine-based exercise. In addition, it's much harder to cheat with an elastic resistance exercise because you can't use momentum to jerk the weight into position. In contrast to pulley- and machine-based resistance, elastic resistance offers inherent and smoother eccentric resistance during the return phase of the movement, thus stimulating the anti-gravity function of muscles. Finally, elastic bands also allow for higher-speed movements and plyometric exercises, whereas isotonic resistance and machines do not.

Disadvantages

While elastic resistance training has several advantages, it does have some disadvantages. Unfortunately, elastic bands and tubing do occasionally break. While they are more subject to wear and tear than isotonic weights, advances in the manufacturing of elastic resistance products has lengthened their useful life. Care must be taken when using bands to inspect them and avoid sharp objects. Be sure the bands are securely attached so they don't snap and injure you. It is also difficult to quantify the specific amount of resistance of an elastic band compared to an isotonic weight. For example, we can't say that a particular band is equal to a specific amount of resistance as you can with a dumbbell; the force produced by each band depends on how much it is stretched.

Most elastic bands and tubing contain natural latex rubber to which some people have an allergy, marked by redness, swelling, and welts where the skin contacts the band or tubing. Those persons sensitive to latex should use latex-free bands and tubing to avoid allergic reactions. It's reasonable to say, however, that the advantages of elastic resistance outweigh the disadvantages.

Is ERT Functional Training?

Some have said that training with bands is not functional, arguing that the increasing force of the bands is counter to the increasing-decreasing bell-shaped muscular strength curve. Their argument is that the band is at its highest force when the muscle is least able to produce force at the end range. However, research has shown that the strength curve produced by elastic resistance is, in fact, similar to strength curves of isotonic resistance: both produce a bell-shaped curve (figure 1.2). In addition, elastic resistance exercises are not restricted by a single plane of motion as typical isotonic resistances provide. Elastic resistance offers multiple planes of resistance, providing resistance in the *frontal, sagittal,* or *transverse planes* (front and back, left and right, and, at the midsection, top and bottom), offering resistance to both isolated and integrated movements. Elastic resistance is uniquely suited for replicating whole-body, multiple-joint movements of functional activities such as simulated throwing, lifting, or running. Based on the biomechanical and clinical evidence, elastic resistance is definitely ideal for functional training.

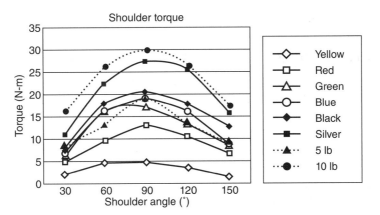

Figure 1.2   Strength curves of isotonic (dumbbells) and elastic resistance (using Thera-Bands of various colors).

Adapted from C.J. Hughes, K. Hurd, A. Jones, and S. Sprigle, 1999, "Resistance properties of Thera-Band tubing during shoulder abduction exercise," *Journal of Orthopaedic & Sports Physical Therapy* 29(7):413-420. Used with permission of JOSPT.

Types of Elastic Resistance Devices

Elastic resistance is available in a variety of devices. Elastic bands are the most popular type, often provided on rolls in widths of three to six inches. Elastic band loops (figure 1.3) are also available; these provide convenient exercise without needing to tie the bands together. These loops come in a variety of thicknesses and lengths and are used for rehabilitation and fitness. Exercise tubing is also available, either with or without attached handles. Tubing with handles is popular in group fitness training.

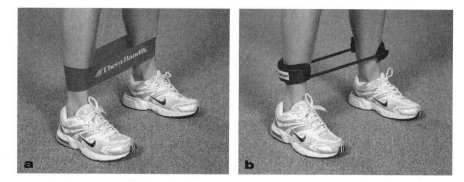

Figure 1.3 Thera-Band elastic loops.

There is little difference between bands and tubing. In general, the same color bands and tubing from the same manufacturer tend to have the same resistance levels at any given percent of elongation. This is because manufacturers generally match the specific amount of elastic product (cross section area) between similarly colored bands and tubing. Be aware, however, that resistance levels do vary among manufacturers. Physiologically and biomechanically, there are no differences between bands and tubing in terms of resistance-training stimulus. The choice between bands and tubing is a matter of personal preference: tubing tends to be preferred for upper extremity exercises, and bands tend to be preferred for lower body exercises.

A benefit of exercising with bands is that you can simply wrap the bands around your hands or stabilize the band with your body rather than attaching it to something (see figure 1.4). Some users prefer to attach handles to the band, however. When wrapped around the hand, tubing has a tendency to dig into the skin and roll over bony areas during movement. Exercise tubing with attached handles helps reduce this problem (figure 1.5). Although not essential, accessories and attachments for the bands and tubing (see figure 1.6 on page 10) can increase the number of exercises you perform. Regardless of the method used to create an attachment point for the elastic, it is vital that you insure the solidity of that connection to prevent injury. In general, however, accessories, such as handles, carabiners, door anchors, and extremity straps are recommended for tubing exercises to avoid hand discomfort. Using door anchors allows exercisers at home to vary the position of the band origin at different locations depending on the exercise.

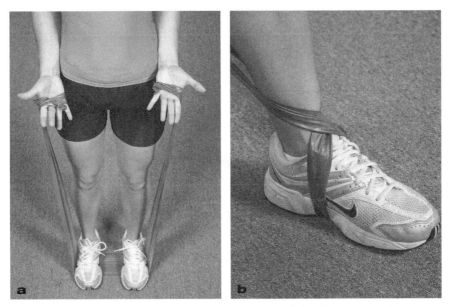

Figure 1.4 Thera-Band *(a)* hand wrapping and *(b)* ankle wrapping.

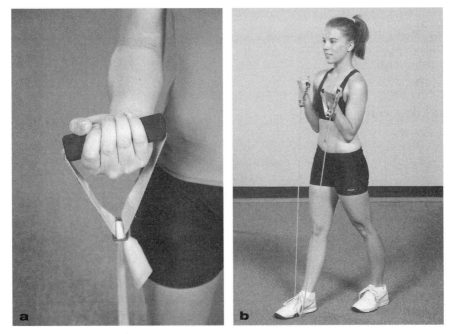

Figure 1.5 Thera-Band *(a)* exercise band and *(b)* tubing with attached handles.

Figure 1.6 Commonly used Thera-Band accessories: *(a)* door anchor, *(b)* extremity strap, *(c)* sports handle, *(d)* assist strap used in the hand, and *(e)* assist strap attached to object.

Safety First

- Inspect the bands or tubing before each use, particularly at the stationary attachment point, and replace if you find any nicks or tears.

- Ensure the security of your stationary attachment point of the elastic band or tubing; for instance, use a firmly closed door. Be sure you are pulling against the natural swing of the door.

- Perform motions slowly and with control; don't let the band or tubing snap back.

- Avoid sharp objects, including jewelry and fingernails, when using bands and tubing.

- Never pull the band or tubing directly toward your face.

- Protect your eyes when performing exercises that may cause the band or tubing to snap back toward your face.

- Don't elongate bands or tubing to more than three times their resting length (for example, never stretch a two-foot band beyond six feet).

- Persons with a latex allergy should exercise with latex-free exercise bands and tubing.

Training and Exercise

Elastic resistance exercise allows you to do the same types of exercises performed on expensive gym equipment, and it allows those exercises to be performed at home or while traveling. As stated previously, research has shown that elastic resistance exercises provide the same physiological benefits and outcomes as exercising with machines. In addition, using ERT frees you from the limitations of gravity, allowing you to isolate muscles and perform the same movements in a totally different way, perhaps becoming more functionally specific as well.

By simply varying the level of resistance, the number of repetitions, and the speed of the exercise, you can individually tailor a strengthening program to meet your needs of weight loss, body toning, general strength and conditioning, or to improve speed, power, and agility for sports.

For example, using higher resistance with fewer repetitions will increase muscle size and power, whereas using a lower resistance with more repetitions may help keep you trim. Choose your volume (sets and repetitions) and your intensity (resistance level or color of band) by your goals. The following "dosing chart" (table 1.3) may be helpful in determining your exercise level. For each goal listed, the second column shows the recommended intensity based on a one repetition maximum effort, and the third column shows the number of repetitions that should be performed using a multiple RM intensity. The multiple RM intensity is the amount of resistance that allows for a specific number of repetitions.

Table 1.3   Thera-Band Dosing Table

Goal	Intensity (% 1RM)	Volume (multiple RM)
Strength and power	85-90	3-6
High-intensity endurance and speed	70-75	10-12
Low-intensity endurance	55-60	20-25

You should use a rating of perceived exertion (RPE) scale to monitor your intensity when exercising with elastic bands or tubing. The Borg scale and OMNI scale (figure 1.7) are two commonly used RPE scales. Use these or other RPE scales to maintain a moderate intensity (12 to 14 on the Borg scale, and 5 to 7 on the OMNI scale). In the 2008 study cited previously, Colado and Triplett showed that the OMNI Scale can be used with ERT to produce strength gains similar to isotonic weights.

Start your program with lighter resistances to emphasize proper form and movements. Perform movements slowly and with control and emphasize the negative (eccentric, or returning) part of the movement. Don't let the band snap quickly back to the resting position. Improper

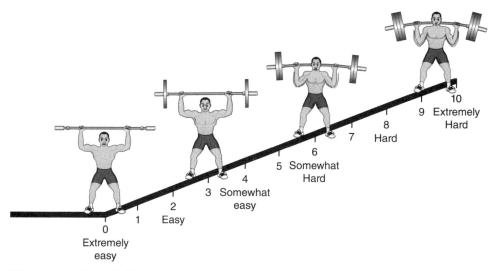

Figure 1.7 OMNI scale of perceived exertion.

From R.J. Robertson, 2004, *Perceived exertion for practitioners: Rating effort with the OMNI picture system* (Champaign, IL: Human Kinetics), 144. Reprinted by permission of the author.

movements often lead to joint injury and pain. Don't forget to balance your exercises by performing exercises for muscles on the front of the body as well as the rear. For example, if you do a bench press, you should also do a seated row to balance the shoulder muscles. It's also essential to breathe properly during resistance exercises; never hold your breath while doing resistance exercises. As with any exercise program, a proper warm-up and cool-down is recommended. Finally, proper posture is very important when performing these exercises.

Progression is the key to strength training programs. Elastic bands and tubing come in a variety of strengths and can be easily changed as your strength progresses. For example, Thera-Band exercise bands and tubing are color coded to help you progressively increase the resistance

Precautions for Beginning an Exercise Program

- Be sure you have your physician's approval for resistance exercise.
- If you have chronic musculoskeletal pain, you should see a physical or occupational therapist before beginning.
- Remember that soreness is to be expected at the beginning of any unaccustomed exercise program, and should subside in a few days.
- You should contact your healthcare provider if you experience severe soreness for more than three days after your workout.

(see figure 1.8). As you gain strength and control, gradually increase the number of exercises you do and the resistance level you use by progressing to the next color band or tubing. You can also progress from isolated movements (see chapter 3), such as a shoulder side raise, to more integrated movements, such as diagonal and rotational throwing motions (see chapter 10), replicating more functional movements.

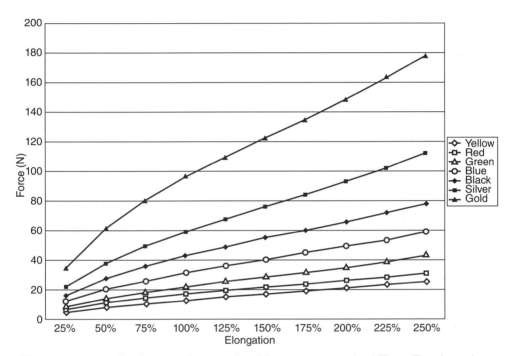

Figure 1.8 Resistance, in pounds of force generated, of Thera-Band products by color and percent of elongation.

Reprinted, by permission, from C. Hughes and P. Page, 2003, Scientific basis of elastic resistance. In *The scientific and clinical application of elastic resistance,* edited by P. Page and T.S. Ellenbecker (Champaign, IL: Human Kinetics), 7. Data from P. Page, A. Labbe, and R. Topp, 2000, "Clinical force production at Thera-Band elastic bands," *Journal of Orthopaedic & Sports Physical Therapy* 30(1): A47-48.

Importance of Posture

Your exercise programs should also be advanced as you improve your strength, stabilization, and coordination. Begin your program by concentrating on isolated movements for single-joint muscle groups such as biceps curls and leg extensions (chapter 3) to build a base of muscular stability and strength. You may then progress to compound movements that involve multiple joints, such as a bench press or leg press (chapters 4 through 6). Next, incorporate functional movements such as a throwing motion or side jump (chapters 7 through 8). Finally, integrate sport-specific exercises to enhance your performance (chapters 10 through 12). This progression is depicted in the ERT Pyramid in figure 1.9.

It's important to maintain good overall body posture before, during, and after each movement, emphasizing proper spinal posture. Even when performing shoulder exercises only, you must have good alignment of the lower back and hips to maintain a stable base for the shoulder muscles to work from. Most of the exercises in this book are performed while standing to help increase activation of the core stabilizers and to improve balance, but different postures can be used within the same movement for a different effect. For example, you will have a lower core activation performing a bench press while lying on a bench than if you do the same exercise while standing or sitting on an exercise ball. We prefer to use a well-balanced standing posture with the exercises in this book (see figure 1.10). In general, you should maintain a neutral lumbar and cervical spine; keep the shoulders back and down; slightly contract the abdominals, pulling the navel inwards; keep knees soft, not locked; and keep wrists in a neutral position. A balanced training posture promotes overall body stability and thus improves activation of the core.

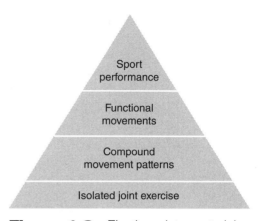

Figure 1.9 Elastic resistance training pyramid.

Figure 1.10 Balanced posture.

Quality Versus Quantity

Because these exercises increase the demand on the whole body as well as the joint they isolate, the body may be more prone to fatigue and compensatory movement patterns elsewhere in the body. With that in mind, we advocate exercises performed for quality rather than quantity. Remember that strength training is based not just on building muscle, but also on building the motor memory (nervous system messages) for correct movement patterns; therefore, proper posture and movement is much more important than overall volume of training.

While overall posture is key, it's important to remember that the position of the band in relation to the person exercising will have a significant effect on the exercise itself. In particular, the stationary position of the band's attachment point and the subsequent line of pull or the angle of resistance will affect the overall strength curve of the exercise, as well as the stabilization requirements of the exercise. In general, the resistance band should be within the plane of movement and parallel to the muscle fibers performing the movement. During a biceps curl, for example, the exercise band should be within the sagittal plane, parallel to the fibers of the biceps (see figure 1.11). For a more detailed explanation of the

Figure 1.11   *(a)* Correct versus *(b)* incorrect technique for the biceps curl.

How to Care for Your Band

- Don't store your band in direct sunlight or heat, and avoid extremes of temperature.
- Your band can be washed with gentle soap and water.
- Dry bands by laying them flat.
- Use handles (available separately) if you have trouble gripping the band.
- Don't overstretch your band beyond normal exercise use.
- Inspect for tears and nicks before use and replace band if needed.

biomechanics and positioning with elastic resistance training, see Page and Ellenbecker's *The Scientific and Clinical Application of Elastic Resistance* (Human Kinetics, 2003).

Elastic bands can be used as part of a well-rounded physical activity program for all ages. Children and older adults can benefit from strength, balance, or flexibility activities using bands. The following chapters provide specific exercises to strengthen all major muscle groups and functional activities. The target muscle is listed with each exercise, as well as instructions and tips for proper movements. Be sure you can perform the movement properly before adding resistance. Most importantly, use a resistance that allows you to complete your target repetitions without excessive fatigue or movement substitution. Choose your repetitions and resistance level (volume and intensity) based on your goals (see table 1.2). Most of the exercises in this book are performed while standing to help increase activation of the trunk and to improve balance. The level of the exercise reflects the difficulty and amount of muscle activation required.

Stretching Exercises

Warming up before and cooling down after exercise are important components of any training program. Until recently, stretching was generally considered the best form of preexercise warm-up to reduce injury and improve performance. Research, however, has shown that stretching before exercise does not necessarily reduce injury and may actually hinder performance. Today, an active warm-up involving brisk activity using targeted muscles through their full range of motion is advocated. No definitive research proves that stretching prevents injury, but it remains a popular technique to improve range of motion and functional mobility, particularly if done after exercise as part of the cool-down.

Elastic resistance can be used to assist with many types of stretching programs. Exercises that involve prestretch contraction stretching can be especially beneficial. By performing a contraction of the muscle before you stretch it, you will more effectively stretch the muscle. Research has shown that a prestretch contraction is more effective at increasing muscle length and joint range of motion than a static stretch. Prestretch contraction stretching is easily accomplished through the use of elastic resistance: you contract the muscle against the resistance of the band and follow it with a slow stretch to increase the length of the muscle and increase the range of motion. For example, contracting the hamstrings against elastic resistance prior to stretching it will result in more range of motion at the hip. A prestretch contraction helps muscles relax neurologically and also increases the temperature of the muscle, making it more pliable and easier to stretch.

There are several variations of prestretch contraction stretching based on proprioceptive neuromuscular facilitation (PNF) techniques. PNF was developed many years ago by physical therapists as a rehabilitation technique for patients with neurological injuries such as strokes. PNF is a system of exercise that takes advantage of the neurological control of muscles through *proprioception* (the unconscious awareness of joint position and movement). Using both manual and external resistance, therapists use various PNF techniques to increase muscle strength, improve movement patterns, and restore muscle length. Recently, some muscle-lengthening PNF techniques have been used as part of nonrehabilitation stretching programs. Athletes in particular have been using these techniques as part of their warm-ups.

The most popular PNF muscle lengthening technique type, hold-relax stretching, involves taking the joint to the end range of motion, maximally elongating the muscle to be stretched. The muscle is then contracted with no joint movement, or isometrically, for approximately 5 seconds. The slack at the end range is taken up, and a new stretch position is held for between 10 and 30 seconds. This process is repeated three or four times. Similarly, PNF contract–relax stretching involves moving the joint (contracting the muscle) through its entire range of motion before returning to the end stretch position.

The resistance level of the band is important to consider when performing PNF stretching techniques. Choose a resistance level that gives you a comfortable stretch but allows you to contract the muscle or move the joint. Although there will be some discomfort associated with stretching tight muscles, it should not be painful. Finally, remember to breathe normally while stretching; do not hold your breath while stretching.

The following exercises target various regions of the body and can be used as part of an overall stretching program. Tightness in these muscles is common and may lead to muscle imbalances.

Upper Trapezius Stretch

Begin with one end of the band under your foot. Grasp the other end of the band and stretch the band with the hand on the side to be stretched. With your other hand, grasp the side of your head and bend your neck away from the side to be stretched *(a)*. Keeping your elbow straight, shrug your shoulder upward, pulling the band toward the ceiling, and inhale *(b)*. Hold for 2 to 6 seconds, then slowly allow the band to return the shoulder to the starting position as you exhale. Hold the stretch on the band for an additional 10 to 30 seconds.

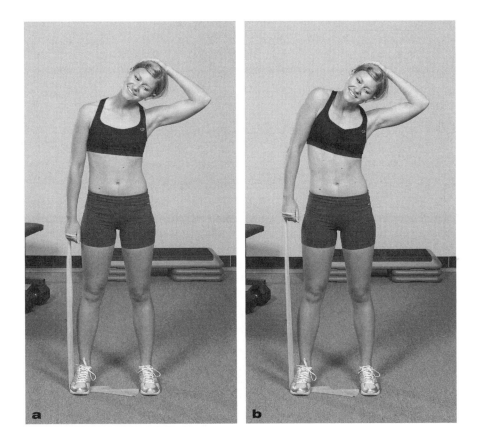

Pectoralis Major Stretch

Attach the ends of a looped band securely to a sturdy object behind you. Stand with your shoulder and elbow bent to 90 degrees. Place the middle of the loop around your elbow and allow the band to stretch the front part of the shoulder (a). Keeping your elbow bent, gently pull your shoulder inward against the band as you inhale (b). Hold for 2 to 6 seconds, then slowly allow the band to return the shoulder to the starting position as you exhale. Hold the stretch on the band for an additional 10 to 30 seconds.

Hip Flexor (Iliopsoas) Stretch

Attach the ends of a looped band securely to a sturdy object near the floor, such as a table leg. Lie on your back on a table or bench with your leg hanging over the edge *(a)*. Attach the looped band around the thigh and gently flex your hip upward against the taut band as you inhale *(b)*. Hold for 2 to 6 seconds, then slowly allow the band to return the leg to the starting position as you exhale. Hold the stretch on the band for an additional 10 to 30 seconds.

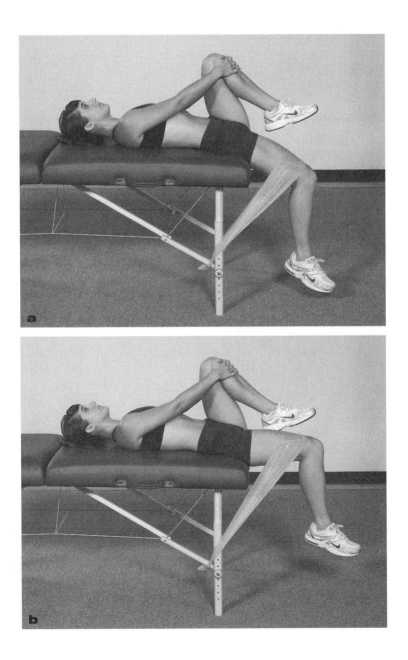

Adductor (Groin) Stretch

Attach the ends of a looped band securely to a sturdy object near the floor. Attach the looped band around the foot on the side to be stretched. Begin sitting with legs spread apart and knees straight, on a slight diagonal from the point of attachment *(a)*. Gently pull your leg inward against the taut band as you inhale *(b)*. Hold for 2 to 6 seconds, then slowly allow the band to return the leg to the starting position as you exhale. Hold the stretch on the band for an additional 10 to 30 seconds.

Piriformis Stretch

Lie with one knee (on the side to be stretched) bent over the opposite knee. Loop the band around the knee to be stretched and grasp the ends of the loop with the hand opposite the side to be stretched *(a)*. Keep the band taut while gently pushing the top knee into the band as you inhale *(b)*. Hold for 2 to 6 seconds, then slowly allow the band to return the leg to the starting position as you exhale. Hold the stretch on the band for an additional 10 to 30 seconds.

Quadriceps Stretch

Attach the ends of a looped band securely to a sturdy object near the floor. Lie on your back on a bench or table with your leg hanging over the edge with the band behind it *(a)*. Attach the looped band around the shin and gently extend your knee against the taut band as you inhale *(b)*. Hold for 2 to 6 seconds, then slowly allow the band to return the leg to the starting position as you exhale. Hold the stretch on the band for an additional 10 to 30 seconds.

Hamstring Stretch

Lie on your back with the looped band around the foot or ankle on the side to be stretched. Keep your opposite knee flexed. Extend the leg upward and grasp the ends of the band, pulling the leg toward your head *(a)*. Gently push your extended leg downward against the band, keeping your knee straight *(b)*. Hold for 2 to 6 seconds, then slowly allow the band to return the leg to the starting position as you exhale. Hold the stretch on the band for an additional 10 to 30 seconds.

Iliotibial Band Stretch

Attach the ends of a looped band securely to a sturdy object near the floor. Lie on a bench or table on the side opposite the leg being stretched with that hip flexed and the leg to be stretched hanging over the edge *(a)*. Attach the looped band around the knee or thigh and gently lift your leg against the taut band as you inhale *(b)*. Hold for 2 to 6 seconds, then slowly allow the band to return the leg to the starting position as you exhale. Hold the stretch on the band for an additional 10 to 30 seconds.

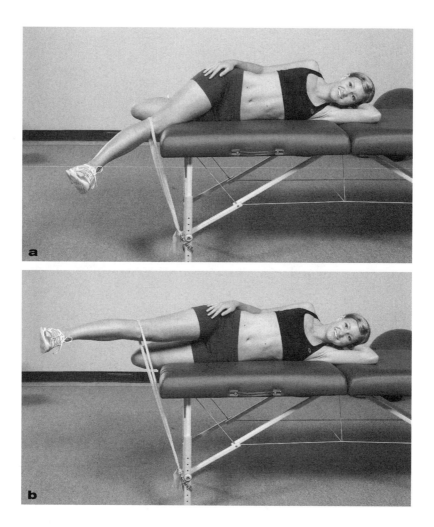

Gastrocnemius and Soleus Stretch

Begin sitting with your knees extended and loop the middle of the band around the foot of the side to be stretched. Grasp the ends of the band, pulling the foot toward your head *(a)*. Gently push your foot downward against the band, keeping your knee straight *(b)*. Hold for 2 to 6 seconds, then slowly allow the band to return the leg to the starting position as you exhale. Hold the stretch on the band for an additional 10 to 30 seconds. To isolate the soleus, perform the same stretch with the knee slightly bent rather than straight.

PART II

Elastic Resistance Training for Stability, Strength, and Power

Joint Isolation Exercises

Isolated joint exercises are probably the most popular form of elastic resistance exercise. These exercises generally involve single joints moving in one direction and are used to target specific muscles that provide joint stability and prevent overuse injuries.

Individually strong muscles and stable joints often form the base for executing simple, as well as more compound, movements. Any chain is only as strong as its weakest link; this statement applies to kinetic, or movement, chains as well as any other type. A chain of movement is limited by the weakest muscle, or sometimes the least stable joint, in the chain.

In the upper body, elastic resistance is particularly effective for shoulder joint exercises. The elbow, hand, and wrist joints can also be exercised with elastic bands and tubing as well as the lower body joints of the hip, knee, foot, and ankle. Resistance exercises for muscles that provide stability to joints of the upper body, arms and hands, and the lower body follow. Note that, in general, it's a good idea to exercise the same joint on both sides of the body. Here, as elsewhere in the book, exercises should be performed with a standard-length band or tubing, except as otherwise noted.

Lateral Raise
(Deltoids)

Stand with one foot slightly in front of the other with the middle of the band or tubing under the foot. Grasp the two ends of the band and bring them around the outside of the feet *(a)*. Lift the bands out to the side at shoulder level, keeping your elbows straight *(b)*. Slowly return to the start position.

VARIATION

Alternate lifting right and left arms.

TRAINING TIPS

Keep your shoulder blades down; avoid shrugging your shoulders with the movements. Keep your abdominals tight. Keep your wrists straight.

Front Raise

(Deltoids)

Use a staggered step, with one foot slightly in front of the other, and stand on the middle of the band or tubing with one foot. Grasp the ends of the band *(a)* and lift the bands forward to shoulder height, keeping your elbows straight *(b)*. Slowly return.

VARIATION

Alternate lifting right and left arms.

TRAINING TIPS

Keep your shoulder blades down; avoid shrugging your shoulders with the movements. Avoid arching your back; keep it straight. Keep your abdominals tight. Keep your wrists straight.

Scaption
(Rotator Cuff, Deltoids)

Stand with one foot in front of the other and place the middle of the band or tubing under the front foot. Grasp the ends of the band or tubing and bring your arms slightly in front of your body, about 30 degrees *(a)*. Lift the bands out to the side to shoulder height *(b)*. Keep your thumbs up and elbows straight. Slowly return.

VARIATION

Perform the exercise with the thumbs down as if you are emptying a can. Be sure to stop at shoulder height.

TRAINING TIPS

Keep your shoulder blades down; avoid shrugging your shoulders with the movements. Avoid arching your back; keep it straight. Keep your abdominals tight. Keep your wrists straight.

Shoulder Internal Rotation at 0 degrees
(Rotator Cuff)

Securely attach one end of the band to a sturdy object and stand beside it, with your working arm nearest the object *(a)*. Grasp the free end of the band with your elbow by your side, bent 90 degrees, and your forearm parallel to the floor. Pull the band away from the attachment point *(b)* and return slowly.

VARIATION

Place a large pillow between your arm and trunk to increase the abduction of your shoulders while performing the exercise.

TRAINING TIPS

Keep your wrist straight. Keep your elbow bent at 90 degrees; don't extend your elbow or wrist to complete the motion. Keep your trunk stationary; don't rotate your trunk to complete the motion.

Shoulder External Rotation at 0 degrees
(Rotator Cuff)

Securely attach one end of the band to a sturdy object and stand beside it, with your non-working arm nearest the object. Grasp the end of the band with your elbow by your side, bent 90 degrees, and your forearm parallel to the floor *(a)*. Pull the band away from the attachment *(b)*, and return slowly.

VARIATION

Lift your arm so that your shoulder is at a 90-degree angle and keep your elbow at shoulder height. Pull the band away from the attachment, keeping your shoulder and elbow bent 90 degrees.

TRAINING TIPS

Keep your wrist straight. Keep your elbow bent at 90 degrees; don't extend your elbow or wrist to complete the motion. Keep your trunk stationary; don't rotate your trunk to complete the motion.

Serratus Punch
(Serratus Anterior)

Securely attach one end of the band to a sturdy object behind you. Grasp the end of the band at shoulder height with your elbow extended *(a)*. Keep your trunk steady and shift your shoulder forward to punch the end of the band away from the attachment *(b)*. Slowly return.

VARIATION

Perform the exercise while supine by placing the middle of the band around your upper back. Grasp the end of the band at shoulder level and push the band toward the ceiling as you keep your elbow straight.

TRAINING TIPS

Keep your elbow straight throughout the exercise. Don't allow your trunk to rotate during the exercise.

Biceps Curl
(Biceps)

Stand on the middle of the band or tubing with one foot slightly in front of the other. Grasp the ends of the band with your palms up and elbows by your side (*a*). Bend your elbows, lifting the bands upward *(b)*. Slowly return.

VARIATION

Securely attach one end of the band to a sturdy object at shoulder height. Lift your shoulder forward to 90 degrees and grasp the band with your elbow straight. Keeping your shoulder stable, bend your elbow and bring your hand to your shoulder.

TRAINING TIPS

Keep your shoulders and elbows steady. Keep your back straight and don't lean back. Keep your abdominals tight. Keep your wrists straight; don't bend them to complete the motion.

Elbow Extension
(Triceps)

Securely attach the middle of the band to a stationary object above your head. Facing the attachment point, grasp the ends of the band with your elbows bent and by your side *(a)*. Straighten your elbows, keeping them by your side *(b)*. Slowly return.

VARIATION

Stabilize one end of a long band under your back foot. Bring the band up behind your back and grasp it overhead with your shoulder elevated, the elbow bent, and the palm facing up. Push the band upward, extending your elbow.

TRAINING TIPS

Keep your shoulders and elbows steady. Keep your back straight and don't lean forward to complete the exercise. Keep your abdominals tight. Keep your wrists straight.

Wrist Flexion
(Wrist Flexors)

Sit with your knees flexed and secure the ends of the band under one foot. Use the nonworking hand to stabilize your forearm on your thigh. Grasp the middle of the band with the palm up *(a)*. Bend your wrist upward and slowly return *(b)*. After several repetitions, switch to the other arm.

VARIATION
Sit on an exercise ball for more of a challenge.

TRAINING TIP
Keep your elbow in one position during the exercise; don't use your elbow to complete the exercise.

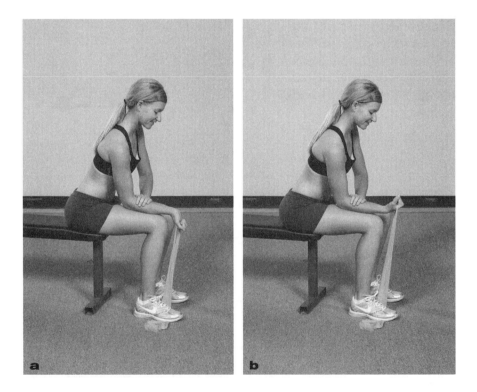

Wrist Extension
(Wrist Extensors)

Sit with your knees flexed and secure the ends of the band under one foot. Use the nonworking hand to stabilize your forearm on your thigh. Grasp the middle of the band with the palm down *(a)*. Bend your wrist upward and slowly return *(b)*. After several repetitions, switch to the other arm.

VARIATION

Hold ends of the bands between your hands, about shoulder-width apart, with your palms facing each other. Extend both your wrists at the same time. Sit on an exercise ball for more of a challenge.

TRAINING TIP

Keep your elbow in one position during the exercise; don't use your elbow to complete the exercise.

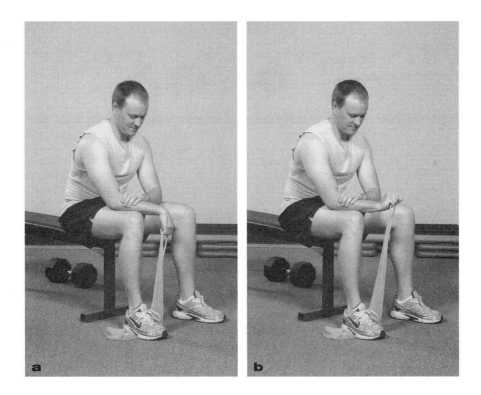

Forearm Supination
(Supinator, Biceps)

While seated, stabilize both ends of the band under your foot, and place your forearm on your knee. Grasp the middle of the band with the palm down *(a)*. Rotate your forearm and turn your palm upward *(b)*. Slowly return.

VARIATION

Hold the ends of the bands between your hands, about shoulder-width apart, with your palms facing each other. Rotate both your forearms at the same time and turn your palms upward. Sit on an exercise ball for more of a challenge.

TRAINING TIP

Keep your elbow in one position during the exercise; don't use your elbow to complete the exercise.

Forearm Pronation
(Pronator Teres)

Sit on a bench with your knees flexed and stabilize the middle of the band under your foot; place your forearm on your knee. Grasp the middle of the band with the palm up and band next to thumb *(a)*. Rotate your forearm and turn your palm downward *(b)*. Slowly return.

VARIATION

Sit on an exercise ball for more of a challenge.

TRAINING TIP

Keep your elbow in one position during the exercise; don't use your elbow to complete the exercise.

Ulnar Deviation
(Forearm Flexors and Extensors)

Sit on a bench and secure the ends of the band under your foot. Grasp the middle of the band with the palm facing inward and elbow by your side with your thumb pointing forward *(a)*. Keeping your elbow steady, move your wrist backward *(b)*. Slowly return.

VARIATION

Sit on an exercise ball for more of a challenge.

TRAINING TIPS

Keep your elbow in one position during the exercise; don't use your elbow to complete the exercise. Don't extend your shoulder; keep it stationary.

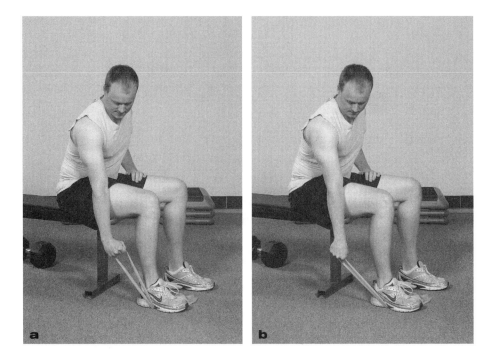

Radial Deviation
(Forearm Flexors and Extensors)

Sit on a bench with knees flexed and secure the ends of the band under your foot. With your elbow stabilized on your thighs, grasp the middle of the band with the thumb pointing upward *(a)*. Keeping your elbow steady, move your wrist upward *(b)*. Slowly return.

VARIATION

Sit on an exercise ball to increase the challenge.

TRAINING TIP

Keep your elbow in one position during the exercise; don't use your elbow to complete the exercise.

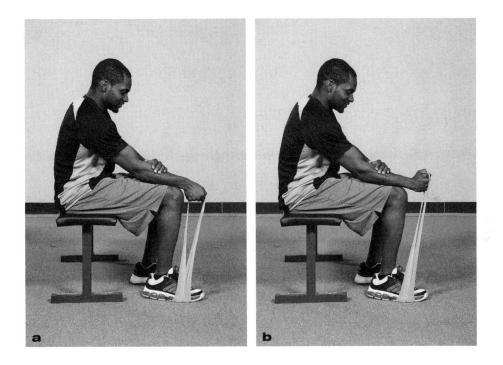

Hip Internal Rotation

(Hip Rotators)

Secure both ends of the band to a stationary object. Sit in a chair or on a bench with the attachment point on the opposite (nonworking) side and loop the middle of the band around your ankle *(a)*. Rotate your lower leg outward against the band *(b)*. Slowly return.

VARIATION

Secure both ends of the band to a stationary object near the floor. With the attachment point on the opposite side, loop the middle of the band around the ankle. In a half-kneeling position (knee up on working side), rotate your lower leg outward and across the floor, pulling the band away from the attachment. Slowly return.

TRAINING TIPS

Avoid arching your back; keep it straight. Avoid bending your hip.

Hip External Rotation
(Hip Rotators)

Secure both ends of the band to a stationary object. Sit in a chair or on a bench with the attachment point on the same (working) side and loop the middle of the band around your ankle *(a)*. Rotate your lower leg inward against the band *(b)*. Slowly return.

VARIATION

Secure both ends of the band to a stationary object near the floor. With attachment on the working side, loop the middle of the band around the ankle. In a half-kneeling position (knee on working side up), rotate your lower leg inward and across the floor, pulling the band away from the attachment point. Slowly return.

TRAINING TIPS

Avoid arching your back; keep it straight. Avoid bending your hip.

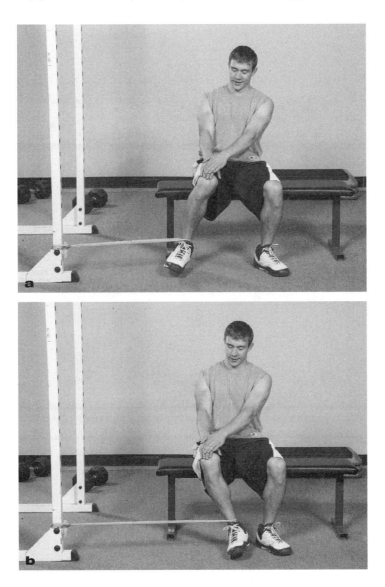

Hip Flexion
(Iliopsoas)

Secure both ends of the band to a stationary object near the floor. Loop the middle of the band around the ankle *(a)*. Face away from the attachment point and slowly swing the leg forward, keeping the knee straight *(b)*.

VARIATION

Loop the middle of the band around your ankle. Step on the band with the other (nonworking) foot and grasp the ends of the band in your hand. Keeping your knee straight, slowly swing your leg forward. Slowly return. Stand on a foam pad for increased challenge.

TRAINING TIPS

Avoid arching your back; keep it straight. Keep the abdominals tight.

Hip Extension
(Gluteus Maximus)

Secure both ends of the band to a stationary object near the floor. Loop the middle of the band around the ankle *(a)*. Face the attachment point and slowly swing the leg backward, keeping the knee straight *(b)*. Slowly return.

VARIATION

Loop the middle of the band around your ankle. Step on the band with the other (nonworking) foot and grasp the ends of the band in your hand. Keeping your knee straight, slowly swing your leg backward. Slowly return. Stand on a foam pad for increased challenge.

TRAINING TIPS

Avoid extending your back; keep it straight. Keep the abdominals tight.

Hip Abduction
(Gluteus Medius)

Secure both ends of the band to a stationary object near the floor. Loop the middle of the band around the ankle *(a)*. Slowly swing your leg outward, keeping the knee straight *(b)*. Slowly return.

VARIATION

Loop the middle of the band around your ankle. Step on the bands with the other (nonworking) foot and grasp the ends of the band in your hand. Keeping your knee straight, slowly swing your leg outward. Slowly return. Stand on a foam pad for increased challenge.

TRAINING TIP

Avoid arching your back; keep it straight. Keep the abdominals tight.

Hip Adduction
(Hip Adductors)

Secure both ends of the band to a stationary object near the floor. Loop the middle of the band around the ankle *(a)*. Slowly swing your leg across your body, keeping the knee straight *(b)*. Slowly return.

VARIATION

Loop the middle of the band around your ankle. Step on the bands with the other (non-working) foot and grasp the ends of the band in your hand Keeping your knee straight, slowly swing your leg across your body. Slowly return. Stand on a foam pad for increased challenge.

TRAINING TIPS

Avoid arching your back; keep it straight. Keep the abdominals tight.

a

b

Knee Flexion
(Hamstrings)

Secure both ends of the band to a stationary object. Sit on a bench facing the attachment point. Loop the middle of the band around the ankle *(a)*. Flex your knee toward your buttocks *(b)* and slowly return.

VARIATION

Secure both ends of the band to a stationary object about knee height. Lie on your stomach with your head away from the attachment point. Loop the middle of the band around one ankle. Begin with your knee bent and flex your knee against the band, pulling it toward your buttocks. Slowly return.

TRAINING TIPS

Keep your back straight and your abdominals tight. Avoid arching your back.

Knee Extension
(Quadriceps)

Secure both ends of the band to a stationary object. With your back to the attachment point, sit on a bench and loop the middle of the band around the ankle and foot *(a)*. Extend your knee *(b)* and slowly return.

VARIATION

Secure both ends of the band to a stationary object about knee height. Lie on your stomach with your head closest to the attachment point. Loop the middle of the band around one ankle. Begin with your knee bent and extend your knee against the band until it reaches the floor. Slowly return.

TRAINING TIPS

Keep your back straight and your abdominals tight. Avoid arching your back.

Terminal Knee Extension
(Quadriceps, Vastus Medialis)

Make a loop with your band and securely attach both ends to a sturdy object at knee height. Facing the attachment point, place your bent knee inside the loop and take up the slack *(a)*. Slowly straighten and bend your knee, stretching the band as you extend your knee *(b)*.

VARIATION
Perform the exercise standing on only one leg. Stand on a foam pad for increased challenge.

TRAINING TIPS
Be sure the band is wrapped above your knee joint. Don't hyperextend your knee.

Dorsiflexion
(Tibialis Anterior)

Sit on the floor with both knees extended. Loop the middle of the band around one foot and grasp the ends of the band. Press your other (nonworking) foot down onto the band to stabilize the band *(a)*. Lift the foot of the working ankle toward your head against the resistance of the band *(b)*. Slowly return.

VARIATION

Perform the exercise while sitting with your knees bent. Loop the middle of the band around one foot and stabilize the band under your other foot. Lift the ankle to be exercised upward. Slowly return.

TRAINING TIP

Keep your knee from moving excessively to complete the exercise.

Plantar Flexion
(Gastrocnemius and Soleus)

Sit on the floor with both knees extended. Loop the middle of the band around one foot and grasp the ends of the band *(a)*. Push the foot down against the resistance of the band *(b)*. Slowly return.

VARIATION

Perform the exercise while sitting in a chair or on an exercise ball. Bend the knee slightly to exercise the soleus muscle.

TRAINING TIP

Keep your knee from moving excessively to complete the exercise.

Inversion
(Tibialis Posterior)

Sit on the floor with one knee extended. Loop the middle of the band around the foot on the extended leg; cross the other (nonworking) leg over the extended leg. Wrap the ends of the band around the top foot and grasp the ends of the band *(a)*. Turn your foot inward away from the band *(b)*. Slowly return.

VARIATION

Sit with the foot to be exercised over the opposite knee. Loop the middle of the band around the foot and stabilize the ends of band under the foot on the floor. Lift the foot only upward toward your head. Slowly return.

TRAINING TIP

Keep your knee and hip stable; don't rotate your leg to complete the exercise.

Eversion
(Peroneals)

Sit on the floor with both knees extended. Loop the middle of the band around the foot and wrap the ends around your nonworking foot, and grasp the ends of the band *(a)*. Turn your foot outward away from the band *(b)*. Slowly return.

VARIATION

Sit with knees bent and the middle of the band looped around the foot to be exercised. Stabilize the ends of the band under the opposite foot. Turn the foot outward away from the band. Slowly return.

TRAINING TIP

Keep your knee and hip stable; don't rotate your leg to complete the exercise.

4

Chest, Upper Back, and Shoulder Exercises

One of the most overworked areas of the body in strength training is the chest, principally for aesthetic reasons. Unfortunately, few athletes spend time to balance the overworked chest muscles with the upper back muscles. This imbalance can contribute to poor posture as well as shoulder and neck problems. Elastic resistance easily replicates the common exercises performed with traditional strengthening equipment and allows you to perform these exercises while standing, thus making your workouts even more challenging. Strengthening of the chest and upper back may help prevent or rehabilitate shoulder injuries as well as neck injuries. In addition, sport-specific training of the chest and upper back is important in overhead and throwing sports such as baseball, softball, tennis, and volleyball. Strengthening the chest and upper back has functional implications for carrying objects and for pushing and pulling movements. It's important to strengthen opposing muscle groups for muscle balance; for example, be sure to balance chest exercises with upper back exercises.

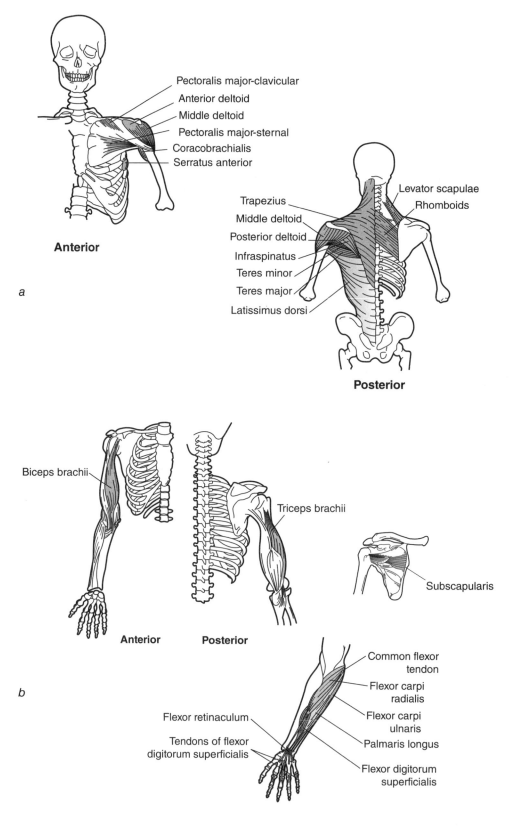

Muscles of the *(a)* chest and upper back, anterior and posterior views, and *(b)* of the shoulder and arm.

Chest Press
(Pectoralis Major, Anterior Deltoid)

Secure the middle of the band to a stationary object at or slightly above shoulder height. Face away from the attachment point. Use a staggered step with one leg slightly in front of the other. Grasp the ends of the band at shoulder height with your elbows bent *(a)*. Extend your elbows, pushing the bands forward *(b)*. Slowly return.

VARIATION

Vary the height of the attachment of the band for an incline (lower attachment height) or decline (higher attachment height) press.

TRAINING TIPS

Keep your shoulder blades down; avoid shrugging your shoulders with the movements. Avoid arching your back; keep it straight. Keep your abdominals tight. Keep your wrists straight.

Chest Fly
(Pectoralis Major, Anterior Deltoid)

Secure the middle of the band to a stationary object at shoulder height. Face away from the attachment point. Use a staggered step with one leg slightly in front of the other. Grasp the ends of the band at shoulder height with your elbows straight or nearly straight (a). Pull the bands inward with your palms facing each other (b). Slowly return.

VARIATION

Vary the height of the attachment of the band for an incline (lower attachment point) or decline (higher attachment point) fly.

TRAINING TIPS

Keep your back straight and abdominals tight. Avoid arching your back or rounding your shoulders. Keep your wrists straight.

Push-Up
(Pectoralis, Triceps)

Assume the push-up position on the floor. Stabilize the ends of the band under each hand and stretch the middle around the shoulder blades *(a)*. Perform a push-up against the resistance of the band *(b)*.

VARIATION
Perform the push-up on your toes or knees.

TRAINING TIPS
Avoid arching your back; keep it straight. Avoid letting your hips sag.

Supine Pullover
(Pectoralis, Latissimus Dorsi)

Securely attach the ends of the band to a stationary object near the floor. Lie on your back with your knees bent. Extend your arms overhead with your elbows straight and grasp the middle of the band *(a)*. Keep the elbows straight and pull the band down to the hips *(b)*. Slowly return.

VARIATION

Alternate left and right arms.

TRAINING TIPS

Avoid arching your back; keep it straight. Keep your elbows and wrists straight.

Dynamic Hug
(Serratus Anterior)

While standing, wrap the middle of the band around your shoulder blades, pass the ends over your arms, and grasp them at or slightly below chest height. Slightly abduct your shoulders and bend your elbows *(a)*. Bring both hands together across the front of your body as if you were hugging someone *(b)*. Slowly return.

TRAINING TIPS

Be sure to keep your elbows flexed and to separate your shoulder blades at the end of the exercise. Keep your neck in a neutral position; don't allow your head to move forward.

Seated Row
(Rhomboids, Middle Trapezius)

Sit on a bench and secure the middle of the band to a stationary object in front of you. Grasp the ends of the band with your elbows extended in front *(a)* and pull the bands toward your lower ribs, bending your elbows *(b)*. Slowly return.

VARIATION

Vary the height that you pull the bands to, such as hip height. Sit on an exercise ball for increased challenge.

TRAINING TIPS

Avoid arching your back; keep it straight. Keep the abdominals tight. Keep your wrists straight.

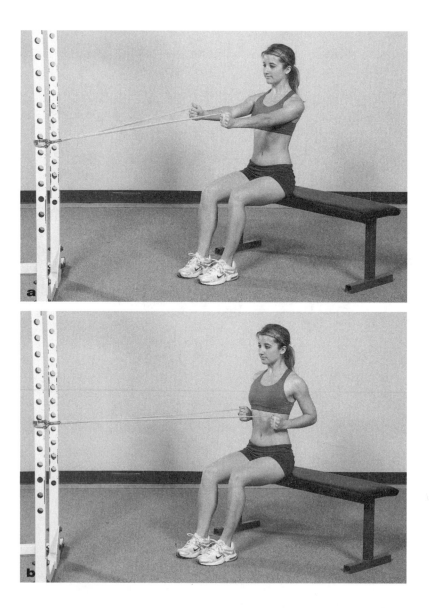

Reverse Fly
(Rhomboids, Middle Trapezius)

Secure the middle of the band to a stationary object at shoulder height. Face the attachment point. Using a staggered step with one leg slightly in front of the other, grasp the ends of the band at shoulder height with your elbows straight *(a)*. Keep your elbows straight and pull the ends of the band outward *(b)*. Slowly return.

VARIATION

Vary the height of the attachment of the band for an incline (lower attachment point) or decline (higher attachment point) fly.

TRAINING TIPS

Keep your back straight and abdominals tight. Avoid arching your back or rounding your shoulders. Keep your wrists straight.

Lat Pull-Down
(Latissimus Dorsi)

Secure the middle of the band to a stationary object above shoulder height. Face the attachment point. Using a staggered step with one leg slightly in front of the other, grasp the ends of the band above shoulder height with your elbows extended in front *(a)*. Bend your elbows and bring your hands to your chest, pulling the bands down and back *(b)*. Slowly return.

VARIATION

Begin with elbows straight above shoulder height. Keep your elbows straight while extending your arms downward.

TRAINING TIPS

Avoid arching your back; keep it straight. Keep the abdominals tight and your wrists straight.

Shrug
(Upper Trapezius)

Stand on the middle of a long band or tubing with both feet. Grasp the ends of the band at hip height *(a)*. Keep your elbows straight and shrug your shoulders *(b)*. Slowly return.

VARIATION

Use a staggered step, with one foot in front of the other, and stabilize the middle of the band under your front foot as you pull the band upward.

TRAINING TIPS

Avoid arching your back; keep it straight. Keep the abdominals tight.

Bent-Over Row
(Rhomboids, Middle Trapezius)

Use a staggered step with one leg in front of the other. Stand on the middle of the band or tubing with the front foot. Bend forward at the hips, keeping your back straight. Grasp the end of the band with your elbow straight *(a)*. Pull one end of the band upward by bending the elbow, bringing your hand to your trunk *(b)*. Slowly return.

VARIATION

Perform the rowing exercise by alternating right and left arms.

TRAINING TIPS

Keep your back straight and avoid arching your back or neck. Keep your wrists straight.

Linton External Rotation
(Rotator Cuff, Scapular Stabilizers)

Begin by kneeling with the band or tubing secured under one hand and maintaining tension with the other hand, forearm on your abdomen. Start the exercise by externally rotating the shoulder (a), then abduct and extend the arm simultaneously, pointing your thumb toward the ceiling (b). Hold; then slowly return, first bringing your elbow into your side.

VARIATION

Squeeze your shoulder blades at the top of the movement for more scapular muscle activation.

TRAINING TIPS

Keep your back and neck straight throughout the exercise. Return the band to the start position very slowly.

Bilateral Extension With Retraction
(Rhomboids, Posterior Deltoid)

Securely attach the middle of the band to a sturdy object in front of you. Grasp the ends of the band at hip height with your elbows straight and palms forward *(a)*. Extend your arms backward and pinch your shoulder blades together against the band *(b)*. Slowly return.

VARIATION

Perform the exercise by alternating right and left arms, extending one at a time.

TRAINING TIPS

Keep your back and neck straight; don't lean back to complete the exercise. Keep your elbows straight and palms forward throughout the exercise.

High Row
(Rhomboids, Middle Trapezius)

Secure the middle of the band to a stationary object in front of you at shoulder height. Grasp the ends of the band with your elbows extended *(a)* and pull the bands toward your chest, bending your elbows *(b)*. Slowly return.

VARIATION

Alternate right and left arms.

TRAINING TIPS

Avoid arching your back; keep it straight. Keep your abdominals tight. Keep your wrists straight.

Upright Row
(Upper Trapezius, Deltoid)

Stand with both feet on the middle of a long band or tubing. Grasp the ends of the band at hip height *(a)* and pull upward toward your chin, bending your elbows *(b)*. Slowly return.

VARIATION

Use a staggered step, with one foot in front of the other, and stabilize the middle of the band under your front foot as you pull the band upward.

TRAINING TIPS

Avoid arching your back; keep it straight. Keep your abdominals tight.

Overhead Press
(Deltoids, Upper Trapezius)

Use a staggered step, with one foot in front of the other, and stabilize the middle of the band or tubing under your back foot. Grasp the ends of the band with your palms forward and your elbows at shoulder height *(a)* and lift the bands overhead *(b)*. Slowly return.

VARIATION

Stand with both feet on the middle of a long band as you push the band overhead.

TRAINING TIPS

Avoid shrugging your shoulders with the movements. Avoid arching your back; keep it straight. Keep your abdominals tight.

Diagonal Flexion: PNF
(Deltoids, Rotator Cuff)

Securely attach one end of the band to a sturdy object near the floor. Stand with your nonworking side next to the attachment point *(a)*. Grasp the other end of the band and pull the band up and away from the attachment point, crossing your body as if you were drawing a sword *(b)*. Keep your elbow straight. Slowly return.

VARIATION

Use two bands and perform the motions with both arms at the same time.

TRAINING TIPS

Keep your back straight and don't rotate your trunk to complete the motion. Keep your abdominals tight.

Diagonal Extension: PNF
(Pectorals, Rotator Cuff)

Securely attach one end of the band to a sturdy object above your head. Stand with your working arm next to the attachment point and grasp the other end of the band *(a)*. Pull the band down and away from the attachment point, keeping your elbow straight and crossing the body as if you were throwing a ball *(b)*. Slowly return.

VARIATION

Use two bands and perform the exercise with both arms at the same time.

TRAINING TIPS

Keep your back straight and don't rotate your trunk to complete the motion. Keep your abdominals tight.

Shoulder External Rotation With Retraction
(Rotator Cuff, Rhomboids)

Use a looped band or create a loop by tying the ends of a band together. Begin with the loop around the outside of both hands, your elbows by your sides, and your forearms parallel to the ground *(a)*. Slowly move your forearms outward and squeeze your shoulder blades together *(b)*. Slowly return.

TRAINING TIPS

Keep your elbows by your sides and your forearms parallel to the ground. Keep your wrists and your back straight.

Dip
(Lower Trapezius, Triceps)

Sit on a bench with your hands on the edge of the seat. Stretch the middle of the band behind your neck and over your shoulders and secure the ends under your hands with your elbows straight. Hold the band ends in your hands and scoot forward, lowering your hips off the bench *(a)*. Keeping your feet stationary, press yourself back and up against the resistance of the band, returning your elbows to straight *(b)*.

VARIATION

Secure the middle of the band overhead. Stand with one foot slightly in front of the other. Grasp the ends of the band with elbows bent and push downward, extending your elbows. Hold and slowly return.

TRAINING TIP

Keep your back straight and abdominals tight.

Shoulder Wall Walk
(Rotator Cuff, Lower Trapezius)

Loop the band around your forearms just below your wrists. Stand near a wall and, with elbows bent, place your forearms on the wall at or just below shoulder height *(a)*. "Walk" your forearms up and down the wall near shoulder height, keeping the distance between your elbows narrower than that between your hands *(b)*.

VARIATION

"Walk" your forearms to the left and right side.

TRAINING TIPS

Don't allow your head or chest to touch the wall. Keep your neck and back straight throughout the exercise. Don't extend your neck. Don't shrug your shoulders.

Shoulder Monster Walk
(Serratus Anterior)

Loop the band around your forearms just below your wrists. Get on your hands and knees with your hands in line with your shoulders and elbows straight *(a)*. While keeping your elbows straight, lift one hand and move it to the side *(b)*. Return the hand to the starting position and repeat on the opposite side.

VARIATION

Perform the exercise moving your hands forward and backward on the floor.

TRAINING TIPS

Keep your back and neck straight throughout the exercise. Don't extend your neck. Keep your elbows straight.

5

Abdominal, Core, and Low Back Exercises

Body-weight resistance is the most common mode of strengthening the abdominals and low back. Adding external resistance such as an elastic band may increase the training stimulus to these areas, particularly in programs whose progress has stalled. The abdominal and core region is a key area for whole-body stabilization and sports performance, most likely because of its ability to generate or transmit forces between the lower and upper extremities. All functional activities of the extremities have some contribution of the core in terms of force production or stabilization. Therefore, core strengthening is vital to performance enhancement in all sport and functional activities. In addition, the abdominal and low back regions are important areas for prevention and rehabilitation of low back pain.

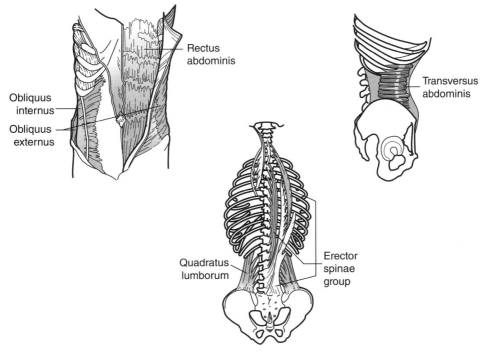

Muscles of the abdomen and low back.

Abdominal Crunch

(Abdominals)

Securely attach the middle of the band to a stationary object near the floor. Lie on your back with your knees bent. Grasp the ends of the band with your hands close together and extend your arms *(a)*. Keeping your elbows straight, curl the trunk upward *(b)*. Be sure to lift the shoulder blades off the floor. Slowly return.

VARIATION

Begin the movement with the arms extended overhead. Pull your arms down while simultaneously performing the curl-up.

TRAINING TIPS

Keep your neck straight; avoid protracting your head. Keep your elbows straight.

Oblique Curl-Up
(Oblique Abdominals)

Securely attach the middle of the band to a stationary object near the floor. Lie on your back with your knees bent. Grasp the ends of the band with your hands close together and extend your arms *(a)*. Keeping the elbows straight, curl your trunk upward while you rotate one of your shoulders toward the opposite knee *(b)*. Lift one shoulder blade off the floor. Slowly return.

VARIATION

Begin the movement with arms your extended overhead. Pull one arm down over the head toward the opposite knee while simultaneously performing the oblique curl-up.

TRAINING TIPS

Keep your neck straight; avoid protracting your head. Keep your elbows straight.

Lower Abdominal Crunch
(Lower Abdominals)

Lie on your back with your hips and knees flexed. Stretch the band over your knees and cross it underneath you. Secure each end of the band under your hands on the floor *(a)*. Lift your knees upward, lifting your hips off the floor *(b)*. Slowly return.

VARIATION

Perform the lower abdominal crunch with knees straight. Stretch the band around your feet and push your legs upward, lifting your hips off the floor.

TRAINING TIP

Avoid arching your back or flexing your hips.

Kneeling Crunch
(Abdominals)

Securely attach the middle of the band to a sturdy object above and in front of you. Assume a half-kneeling position with one knee up. Grasp the ends of band in front of you *(a)*. Curl your trunk downward, rounding your back against the resistance of the band *(b)*. Slowly return.

VARIATION

Rotate your trunk to one side as you curl downward against the band.

TRAINING TIP

Keep your neck in a neutral position.

Trunk Rotation
(Oblique Abdominals)

Sit with your legs extended at least shoulder-width apart. Stretch the middle of the band around both feet. Grasp both ends of the bands with your arms extended forward (a). Rotate the trunk to one side (b) and return slowly to the other.

VARIATION

Securely attach one end of the band to a stationary object at chest height. Stand in an athletic stance with your knees and hips slightly bent and back straight. Grasp the end of the band with your arms extended forward. Rotate the trunk to one side and slowly return.

TRAINING TIP

Keep your back straight and avoid leaning to one side.

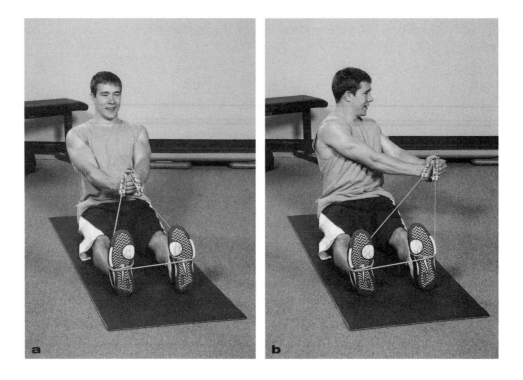

Side Bend
(Quadratus Lumborum)

Stand with your feet shoulder-width apart and your back straight. Secure one end of the band under the feet and grasp the other end of the band by your side with your elbow straight and overhead *(a)*. Lean your trunk away from the band, stretching the band *(b)*. Slowly return.

VARIATION

Stand on one end of the band. Extend an arm overhead, elbow straight, and grasp the other end of the band with your elbow extended down by your side. Lean away, stretching the band, keeping your elbow straight.

TRAINING TIPS

Keep your trunk aligned; don't rotate the trunk. Avoid shifting your hips.

Seated Back Extension
(Multifidus)

Sit with your legs extended. Secure the middle of the band or tubing around both feet. Grasp both ends of the band with your hands at your chest and take up the slack *(a)*. Lean back, stretching the bands as you keep your lumbar spine straight *(b)*. Slowly return.

VARIATION

Perform the exercise with your arms extended straight in front of you.

TRAINING TIP

Keep your lumbar spine in a neutral position (not too rounded or hyperextended).

Standing Back Extension
(Back Extensors, Gluteus Maximus)

Stand in a lunge position with the middle of the band or tubing secured under your front foot. Grasp the ends of the band, keeping your elbows bent and your hands in front of your chest *(a)*. Keep your elbows and hands steady while you extend your back and hips *(b)*. Slowly return.

TRAINING TIPS

Keep your lumbar spine in a neutral position (not too rounded or hyperextended). Be sure the movement occurs in your hips.

Side Bridge
(Quadratus Lumborum)

Lie on your side while holding the band in both hands. Bend your elbow and place it under your shoulder closest to the floor. Keeping your knees and your back straight, lift your hips off the floor until your shoulders and hips are parallel *(a)*. Simultaneously extend your upper arm upward against the band while stabilizing with the opposite arm *(b)*. Slowly return.

VARIATION
Perform the exercise with the knees bent.

TRAINING TIP
Keep your hips and spine aligned; don't let your hips drop or your trunk rotate.

Quadruped Stabilization
(Lumbar Stabilizers)

Begin with knees and hands on the floor. Wrap the middle of the band around the bottom of one foot and stabilize the ends of the band in your hands *(a)*. Keeping your back and neck straight, extend your leg backward against the band, straightening your hip and your knee until they are parallel with the floor *(b)*. Simultaneously extend the opposite arm in front of you. Slowly return. Repeat on the opposite side.

VARIATION

Perform a leg extension only, keeping your hands on the floor.

TRAINING TIPS

Keep your back and neck straight in a neutral position. Don't arch your back or overextend your hips. Don't extend your neck or rotate your back.

Supine Stabilization
(Lumbar Stabilizers)

Lie on your back with one leg straight and the other flexed. Wrap the middle of the band around the bottom of the foot of the straight leg and stabilize the ends of the band in your hands with one arm extended upward *(a)*. Alternate flexing your arms while keeping the elbows straight *(b)*. Keep your back straight and slowly return.

VARIATION

Perform hip flexion and extension (knee straight) against the band simultaneously with the arm flexion.

TRAINING TIPS

Keep your back and neck straight in a neutral position. Don't arch your back.

Hip, Thigh, and Lower-Body Exercises

One of the most important areas of the body to strengthen is the hip and thigh region. As the main link between the lower extremities and the trunk, the hips serve as a stable base for the core (the abdominals and low back region). The hips perform the main role in locomotion, propelling our centers of gravity in walking or running. The gluteal muscles (gluteus maximus and medius) are also important pelvic stabilizers; therefore, the hips and the core are linked in a kinetic chain to transmit and produce force throughout the body. Strong hip muscles are vital to daily activities, particularly during walking or running. In fact, weakness of the gluteal muscles has been linked to chronic back pain and even repetitive ankle sprains. Another vital role of the hip and thigh musculature is to decelerate or slow down body motion, or change the direction of motion. This specialized muscle activity (which often goes untrained) may be a cause for repetitive hip flexor, groin, and hamstring strains in sports. Finally, an imbalance of strength and flexibility between the quadriceps and hamstrings muscles has been linked to knee pain and injury.

Although they are often overlooked, the muscles of the lower leg are also important for balance and agility. In particular, the peroneus longus and tibialis posterior muscles of the ankle provide the stabilization necessary for balance and gait, while the tibialis anterior, gastrocnemius, and soleus provide power and agility during movement.

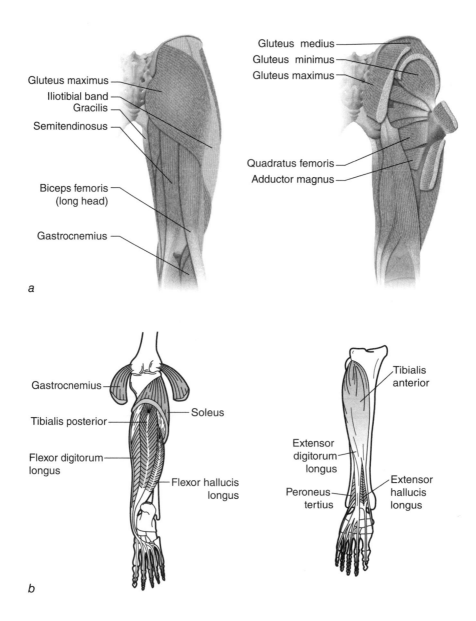

Muscles of the *(a)* hip, thigh, and *(b)* lower extremities.

Hip Lift
(Iliopsoas)

Sit on a bench. Loop the middle of the band around the midthigh and secure both ends of the band under the other foot *(a)*. Lift the upper leg by flexing your hip *(b)* and slowly return.

VARIATION

Secure both ends of the band to a stationary object near the floor. Loop the middle of the band around your ankle. Face away from attachment point and lift the leg upward, keeping the knee bent.

TRAINING TIPS

Avoid arching your back; keep it straight. Keep the abdominals tight.

Bridge
(Gluteus Maximus)

Place the middle of the band on the front of your hips and wrap the ends around your buttocks. Lie on your back with the bands crossed underneath your buttocks. Stabilize each end of the band with your hands on the floor *(a)*. Lift your buttocks off the floor with knees bent, stretching the band against the front of your hips *(b)*. Slowly return.

VARIATION

While in the bridge position with the band stretched, march by alternately lifting your knees.

TRAINING TIP

Keep your hips level at the top of the bridge; don't let your hips or back sag.

Unilateral Bridge
(Gluteus Maximus)

Place the middle of the band on the front of your hips and wrap the ends around your buttocks. Lie on your back with the bands crossed underneath your buttocks. Stabilize each end of the band with your hands on the floor. With your knees bent, lift your buttocks off the floor, stretching the band against the front of your hip *(a)*. Keep one foot off the floor as you raise and lower your buttocks *(b)*.

TRAINING TIP

Keep your hips level at the top of the bridge; don't let your hips or back sag.

Hip Extension (Donkey Kick)
(Gluteus Maximus)

Assume a quadruped position (on hands and knees) and rest on your elbows, keeping your back straight. Secure both ends of the band under your forearms and loop the middle of the band around one foot *(a)*. Keep your knee bent and extend your hip upward against the band *(b)*. Slowly return.

VARIATION

Secure both ends of the band to a stationary object near the floor. Loop the middle of the band around one ankle. Face the attachment and kick your leg backward, keeping your knee bent.

TRAINING TIPS

Avoid arching your back; keep it straight. Keep the abdominals tight.

Side-Lying Hip Lift
(Gluteus Medius)

Lie on your side with your legs extended and loop the band around both ankles
(a). Lift the top leg upward, keeping the knee straight *(b)*. Slowly return.

VARIATION
Loop the band around the knees instead of the ankles to reduce the intensity
of the exercise.

TRAINING TIPS
Keep your back straight. Keep your abdominals tight.

Clam
(Hip Rotators)

Lie on your side with a band looped around your knees, and bend your knees approximately 30 degrees *(a)*. Push the bottom knee into the mat while lifting the top knee against the band *(b)*. Hold and slowly return.

VARIATION

Perform the exercise while lying on your back. Loop the band around your knees and spread your knees apart against the band.

TRAINING TIPS

Be sure there is enough tension on the band to provide resistance throughout the exercise. Don't rotate your trunk to complete the movement.

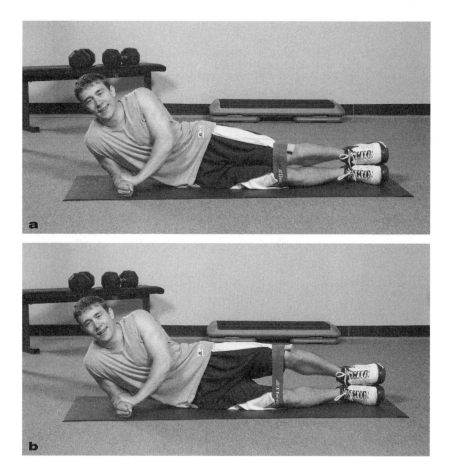

Reverse Clam
(Hip Rotators)

Lie on your side with the band looped around your ankles and your knees bent together *(a)*. Keeping your knees together, rotate your hip inward while lifting your ankle upward against the band *(b)*. Hold and slowly return.

TRAINING TIPS

Be sure there is enough tension on the band to provide resistance throughout the exercise. Don't rotate your trunk to complete the movement.

Good Morning
(Gluteus Maximus, Hamstrings)

Stand on the middle of the band with both feet. Grasp the ends of the band or tubing. Bend down to take up all the slack *(a)*. Keeping your elbows and back straight, slowly return to an upright position against the tension of the band while extending your hips *(b)*.

TRAINING TIPS

Avoid rounding your back; keep it straight. Be sure the movement occurs from the hips, not the back.

Closed-Chain Hip Rotation
(Hip Rotators, Gluteus Maximus, Ankle Stabilizers)

Wrap the middle of the band around your hips, and secure each end in your hands. Stand on the leg of the hip to be exercised and lift the opposite leg. On the nonexercising side, extend your arm forward, stretching the band; keep your other hand at your waist *(a)*. Twist your hips over your weight-bearing leg, pushing the hip of the opposite leg backward into the band *(b)*. Slowly return.

TRAINING TIPS

Keep your shoulders in the same position as you rotate your hips. Don't extend your back or rotate your trunk to complete the movement. Keep your elbow extended.

Lunge
(Gluteus Maximus, Quadriceps)

Stand with one foot on the middle of the band or tubing. Place the other leg behind it with the knee bent. Grasp the ends of the band at chest height with both elbows bent. Keeping your trunk upright, bend your front knee and lower your body by flexing your hips and knees *(a)*. Return to the upright position against the resistance of the band *(b)*.

VARIATION

Perform the lunge exercise with the band held at shoulder height.

TRAINING TIPS

Avoid arching your back; keep it straight. Keep your abdominals tight. Keep your trunk upright at all times.

Lateral Lunge
(Gluteus Medius, Gluteus Maximus, Quadriceps)

Begin with band looped around your lower legs, just above the ankles. Slightly bend your hips and knees into an athletic position *(a)*. Take a step to the side against the resistance of the band as you bend your knees *(b)*. Slowly return.

VARIATION
Change the angle of your side step, either slightly forward or backward of your opposite leg.

TRAINING TIP
Keep your back straight; don't bend or twist at your low back.

Squat
(Gluteus Maximus, Quadriceps)

Stand on the middle of a long band with both feet. Bring the ends of the band around the outside of the feet. Grasp the ends of the band, keeping them at your hips *(a)*. Lower your body into a squat, keeping your back straight *(b)*. Slowly return.

VARIATION

Perform the squat while holding the ends of the bands at shoulder height.

TRAINING TIPS

Avoid arching your back; keep it straight. Keep your abdominals tight.

Barbell Squat
(Gluteus Maximus, Quadriceps)

Loop two pieces of band, one over each end of the barbell, and place the barbell behind your neck and across your shoulders. Secure the ends under your feet so that moderate resistance is present when the squat exercise is in the ascent phase *(a)*. With the barbell in place, lower your body into a squat position and slowly return *(b)*, lifting the barbell with proper form and working with the additional resistance provided by the elastic band.

VARIATION

Perform the front squat against elastic resistance by placing the bar in front of the shoulders, above the chest.

TRAINING TIPS

Keep your back straight throughout the movement. Be sure to have even tension on each end of the bar.

a

b

Single-Leg Squat
(Gluteus Maximus, Quadriceps, Ankle Stabilizers)

Stand on one leg with the middle of the band secured under your foot. Grasp the ends of the band at your hip *(a)*. Perform a one-leg squat, bending your knee 45 to 60 degrees *(b)*. Slowly return. Use external support as needed.

VARIATION

Grasp the end of the band at shoulder height for more resistance.

TRAINING TIPS

Bend your knee straight ahead and align the kneecap with the second toe. Don't let your knee rotate inward or outward. Keep the back and neck straight during the exercise.

Monster Walk
(Gluteus Medius, Gluteus Maximus, Quadriceps)

Loop the band around your thighs, above your knees. Stand with a slight bend in your hips and knees, assuming a ready position *(a)*. Take a step to one side with one leg against the resistance of the band *(b)*. Continue moving in one direction taking multiple steps in a shuffling-type motion.

VARIATION

Step in multiple directions including sideways, diagonally, forward, and backward. Lower the position of the loop to around the ankles for more resistance.

TRAINING TIPS

Keep your back and neck straight throughout the exercise. Don't rotate your trunk or hips to complete the exercise.

Squat Walk
(Gluteus Medius, Gluteus Maximus, Quadriceps)

Loop a band around the lower leg, just above the ankles *(a)*. Walk in a lateral direction, maintaining a flexed position of your trunk and lower body *(b)*.

VARIATION:

Walk in multiple directions, including diagonally, forward, and backward.

TRAINING TIPS

Keep your head up to avoid too much trunk bend. Maintain an athletic posture.

Leg Press
(Gluteus Maximus, Quadriceps)

Lie on your back. Grasp both ends of the band in your hands and loop the middle of the band around one foot *(a)*. Extend your hip and knee simultaneously against the band until the leg is straight and level with your trunk *(b)*. Slowly return.

VARIATION

Sit with knees bent and the middle of a band looped around the bottom of one foot. Lean back onto your elbows and assume a semi-reclined position, stabilizing the ends of the band in your hands. Extend your hip and knee against the band until straight. Slowly return.

TRAINING TIPS

Avoid arching your back; keep it straight. Keep your abdominals tight.

Standing Leg Pull-Through
(Hamstrings, Gluteus Maximus)

Securely attach both ends of the band to a sturdy object in front of you near the floor. Loop the middle of the band around your lower leg above your ankle. Use external support for balance as needed. Begin with your hip flexed in front and your knee extended *(a)*. Pull your leg back against the band, simultaneously flexing your knee and extending your hip *(b)*. Slowly return.

VARIATION

Increase the speed of the repetitions.

TRAINING TIPS

Keep your back and neck straight throughout the exercise. Don't bend your trunk to complete the exercise.

Thera-Band Kick
(Gluteus Maximus, Gluteus Medius, Iliopsoas, Quadriceps, Ankle Stabilizers)

Loop the band around your lower legs, just above the ankles *(a)*. Use external support for balance if needed. Repeatedly kick your leg forward against the band while keeping the knee straight *(b)*. Don't place your foot on the ground between repetitions.

VARIATION

Kick your leg backward as well as out to the side.

TRAINING TIPS

Keep your back and neck straight. Don't lean the trunk to perform the exercise. Be sure there is adequate tension in the band throughout the exercise.

7

Total-Body Exercises

Athletic and functional movements require a strong core consisting of the muscles surrounding the trunk and pelvis: the abdominals and the low back. These muscles must function as movers, stabilizers, and force transducers. Functional strength of the upper extremities (used in actions such as throwing a baseball) is often built initially by the lower body and transferred through the core. While it's important to strengthen these areas individually (see chapter 5), it's just as important to integrate these areas into functional strength through total-body exercises.

Functional training programs should always include total-body exercises that facilitate core stabilization and force transmission between the upper and lower extremities. Elastic resistance exercises can create different vectors of resistance that challenge core stabilization muscles through extremity movement combined with movements such as squats or lunges. In addition, elastic resistance exercises can challenge the muscles involved in whole-body functional movements such as a lift or a push with a step.

Squat With Diagonal Flexion
(Deltoids, Lumbar Stabilizers, Quadriceps)

With your feet about shoulder-width apart, stand on the middle of a long (9 foot) band. Bring the ends around the outside of the feet and cross them in front of your thighs. Grasp both ends of the band near your hips *(a)*. Lower your body into a squat position. At the same time, perform a diagonal flexion by lifting both arms up and out *(b)* at the same time. Slowly return.

VARIATION

Alternate the left and right arm diagonal flexion. Stand on a foam surface for a greater challenge.

TRAINING TIPS

Avoid arching your back; keep it straight. Keep your abdominals tight.

Lunge With Diagonal Flexion
(Deltoids, Lumbar Stabilizers, Quadriceps)

Stand with one foot on the middle of the band. Place the other leg behind it with your knee bent and grasp the ends of the band at hip height *(a)*. Keeping your trunk upright, bend your front knee and lower your body. At the same time, perform the diagonal flexion exercise with both shoulders by lifting both arms up and out *(b)*.

VARIATION

Stand on a foam surface for a greater challenge. Alternate diagonal flexion of the right and left arms during the lunge.

TRAINING TIPS

Avoid arching your back; keep it straight. Keep your abdominals tight. Keep your trunk upright at all times.

Bilateral Chop
(Anterior Trunk, Shoulder)

Securely attach one end of the band to a stationary object above your head. Standing beside the attachment point, assume an athletic stance with hips and knees slightly bent. Grasp the band with both hands over the shoulder closest to the attachment point. Rotate your trunk slightly toward the band *(a)*. Pull the band down to the outside hip with both hands, turning your trunk away from the attachment point *(b)*. Slowly return.

VARIATION

Add more rotation, side bending, or flexion of the trunk to the lifting movement.

TRAINING TIP

Keep your back in neutral at the top of the movement; avoid rounding your back.

Bilateral Lift
(Posterior Trunk, Shoulder)

Securely attach one end of the band to a stationary object near the floor. Begin in an athletic stance with hips and knees slightly bent. With your trunk slightly rotated toward the band, stand to the side of the attachment point and grasp the band with both hands *(a)*. Lift the band over your outside shoulder with both hands, turning your trunk away from the attachment point *(b)*. Slowly return.

VARIATION

Add more rotation, side bending, or flexion of the trunk to the lifting movement.

TRAINING TIP

Keep your back in neutral at the top of the movement; avoid arching your back.

Unilateral Row With Side Bridge
(Rhomboids, Quadratus Lumborum)

Secure one end of the band to a sturdy object near the floor. Lie on your side with your elbow directly under your shoulder. Use your other hand to grasp the band *(a)* and perform a single-arm rowing exercise *(b)* while lifting your hips off the floor and stabilizing the side bridge position. Slowly return.

VARIATION

Perform the side bridge while lifting your arm upward toward the ceiling with your elbow straight until the arm is vertical.

TRAINING TIP

Keep your body in alignment, tensing abdominal muscles and gluteal muscles.

Step Push
(Pectoralis Major, Triceps)

Loop the middle of the band around your shoulder blades and bring the ends under your arms. Grasp both ends of the band at your chest *(a)*. Step forward with one leg while you push the ends of the band forward *(b)*. Slowly return to the starting position.

VARIATION

Step onto a foam surface for a greater challenge. Vary the angle of the pushing movement.

TRAINING TIPS

Tighten your abdominals before and during the exercise. Be sure to keep your back and neck straight as you complete the movement.

Lift Simulation
(Gluteus Maximus, Quadriceps, Lumbar Stabilizers,)

Begin in a staggered-step position. Place the middle of the band under the front foot. Bend your knees and, with your elbows bent, grasp the ends of the band near your knees, keeping your back straight *(a)*. Keeping your elbows bent, use your legs to stand up against the band, as if you were lifting a box, until your knees are straight and your hands are near your hips *(b)*. Slowly return to the starting position.

VARIATION

Stand on a foam surface for a greater challenge.

TRAINING TIPS

Use your legs and keep your arms stationary. Tighten your abdominals before and during the exercise. Be sure to keep your back and neck straight as you complete the movement. Don't round your back.

Step Lift
(Gluteus Maximus, Quadriceps, Lumbar Stabilizers)

Place the middle of the band under one foot and place the other foot behind you. Bend your knees and grasp the ends of the band near your knees, keeping your back straight *(a)*. Keep the foot on the band stationary as you extend your knees and step forward with the other foot. Simultaneously, lift the ends of the band to your hips as if you were lifting a box *(b)*. Slowly return to the starting position.

VARIATION

Step onto foam surface for a greater challenge. Vary the height to which you raise the ends of the band.

TRAINING TIPS

Tighten your abdominals before and during the exercise. Be sure to keep your back and neck straight as you complete the movement. Don't round your back.

Step Incline Press
(Pectoralis Major, Triceps, Deltoids)

Loop the middle of the band around your shoulder blades and bring the ends under your arms. Grasp both ends of the band at your chest *(a)*. Step forward with one leg as you push the ends of the band forward and upward *(b)*. Slowly return to the starting position.

VARIATION

Step onto a foam surface for a greater challenge. Vary the height to which you raise the ends of the band.

TRAINING TIPS

Tighten your abdominals before and during the exercise. Be sure to keep your back and neck straight as you complete the movement. Don't round your back.

Reverse Step Pull
(Rhomboids, Latissimus Dorsi)

Securely attach the middle of the band to a sturdy object in front of you at waist height. Grasp both ends of the band with your arms extended in front. Place one foot in front of the other *(a)*. Step backward with your front foot as you simultaneously pull the bands toward your hips *(b)*. Slowly return.

VARIATION

Stand on a foam surface for a greater challenge. Vary the angle of the origin of the band.

TRAINING TIPS

Tighten your abdominals before and during the exercise. Keep your back and neck straight as you complete the exercise.

Step-Up
(Quadriceps, Gluteus Maximus, Biceps)

Place the middle of the band under one foot on an exercise platform and grasp both ends of the band *(a)*. Step onto the platform with your other foot as you bend your elbows upward against the band *(b)*. Slowly return.

VARIATION

Add a foam surface to the platform for a greater challenge.

TRAINING TIPS

Tighten your abdominals before and during the exercise. Keep your back and neck straight during the exercise. Don't round your back.

Shoulder External Rotation Step
(Rotator Cuff, Rhomboids, Trunk Rotators)

Secure one end of the band to a sturdy object at or slightly above waist height, opposite the side you are exercising. Grasp the other end of the band with your elbow bent at your waist *(a)*. Externally rotate your shoulder, keeping your forearm parallel to the floor and your elbow at your side. Simultaneously step out to the side away from the attachment, rotating your hips and trunk as you point your foot to the side *(b)*. Slowly return.

VARIATION

Step onto foam surface for a greater challenge.

TRAINING TIP

Be sure your hips and trunk rotate together as you step out to the side.

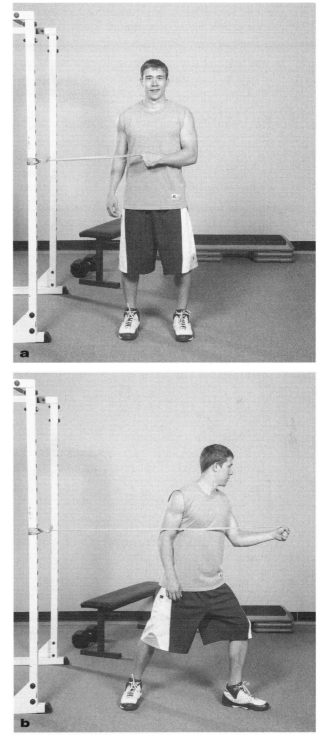

Shoulder Internal Rotation Step
(Rotator Cuff, Pectoralis Major, Trunk Rotators)

Secure one end of the band to a sturdy object at or slightly above waist height on the same side you are exercising. Grasp the other end of the band with your elbow bent and your forearm externally rotated *(a)*. Keep your forearm parallel to the floor and your elbow at your side as you internally rotate your shoulder. Simultaneously, take a step to the side away from the attachment point, rotating your hips and trunk as you point your foot to the side *(b)*. Slowly return.

VARIATION

Step onto a foam surface for a greater challenge.

TRAINING TIP

Be sure your hips and trunk rotate together as you step to the side.

Power, Speed, and Agility Exercises

Elastic resistance can be used to improve the sport performance elements of power, agility, and speed. Power is the ability to exert or produce force in a very short period of time. Agility is the ability to accelerate, decelerate, and change directions quickly while exhibiting good body control, and finally speed may be defined as the rate at which body segments move. Elastic resistance exercise assists in shortening (concentric muscle action), lengthening (eccentric muscle action), and stabilizing (isometric muscle action) muscle to facilitate the development of power, agility, and speed. Several exercise applications of elastic bands and tubing can be used to improve power, agility, and speed. In particular, plyometrics (the rapid stretching and contracting of muscles) is one of the most successful methods of improving speed and power.

Virtually all general physical fitness activities require some combination of all three elements. One of the goals of sport-specific training is to develop these elements to the extent and in a manner that is appropriate for that sport in order to optimize performance and prevent injury. For example, for athletes in a sport like tennis, where explosive multidirectional movements of the lower body are performed repeatedly, training exercises that emphasize power, agility, and speed are necessary staples to allow players to achieve their full potential. Elastic resistance can be used to enhance these important aspects of human performance as they relate to movements common to fitness activity: running, throwing, kicking, swinging, jumping, and other general athletic maneuvers.

Resisted Running
(Lower Extremity Muscle Groups)

Stand with the band wrapped around your waist and the ends secured behind you far enough away not to interfere with running *(a)*. Begin running forward against the resistance of the elastic band *(b)*.

Resisted Backward Running
(Lower Extremity Muscle Groups)

Stand with the band looped around your hips and the ends secured in front of you far enough away not to interfere with running *(a)*. Begin running backward against the elastic resistance *(b)*.

Acceleration
(Lower Extremity Muscle Groups)

Begin in a three-point stance with the band looped around the waist and the ends secured behind you *(a)*. Explode out of your stance and take one step forward *(b)*.

Assisted Sprinting
(Quadriceps, Gastrocnemius, Soleus)

Stand with the band looped around your waist and the ends secured in front, far enough away that they won't interfere with several steps of explosive forward movement *(a)*. There should be moderate tension against the band. Sprint several steps, allowing the band to assist propelling you forward *(b)*. The exercise ends when the tension in the band becomes insignificant.

Reciprocal Arm and Leg Action
(Hip Flexors, Quadriceps, Core Stabilizers)

Secure the ends of the band to a stationary object behind you at about knee level. Wrap the middle of band around one thigh *(a)*. Flex the hip forward, while pulling the arm on the same side backward and punching the opposite arm forward *(b)*. Return and repeat.

Overhead Throw
(Core Muscles, Subscapularis, Pectoralis Major, Latissimus Dorsi)

Securely attach one end of the band to a sturdy object behind you at or above shoulder height. Grasp the other end *(a)* and perform an overhead throwing motion, with follow-through *(b)*, using the resistance from the band to gently overload the muscles used in throwing.

a

b

Underhand Throw
(Anterior Deltoid, Pectoralis Major, Hip Extensors, Quadriceps, Wrist Flexors, Gastrocnemius)

Attach one end of the band to a sturdy object behind you at about waist level. Grasp the other end of the band, with your elbow straight and your arm extended behind you *(a)*. Place one leg behind the other in a staggered stance. As you step forward with the leg opposite the throwing arm, quickly pull the band forward in an underhand motion, keeping your elbow as straight as possible *(b)*.

Bilateral Overhead Throw
(Core Muscles, Latissimus Dorsi, Triceps)

Secure one end of the band to a stationary object overhead and behind you. Stand with your back to the attachment point and grasp the end of band with both arms extended overhead *(a)*. Simulate a soccer throw-in pattern, bending slightly forward at the hips and trunk *(b)*. Combine with a step or twisting motion to work the obliques.

Arm Acceleration Drill
(Rotator Cuff, Scapular Stabilizers)

Secure a band at knee height in front of you. Grab the other end of the band in a starting position (your arm overhead with the thumb pointing backward) *(a)*. Stand far enough from the attachment point that moderate resistance is present. Move your arm forward in a diagonal pattern similar to a throwing motion *(b)*, and work against the resistance of the band as you return to the starting position.

Plyometric Shoulder External Rotation 90/90
(Rotator Cuff, Scapular Stabilizers)

Secure the band to a sturdy object at shoulder height, grasp the other end, and stand facing the attachment point with one shoulder elevated to 90 degrees. Start with the forearm in the vertical position with moderate tension on the band and with elbow bent 90 degrees *(a)*. Quickly move the shoulder until the forearm becomes horizontal *(b)*, and then without pausing, move the arm back to the starting position. Elbow remains bent at 90 degrees throughout the exercise.

Biceps Plyometric Elbow Extension
(Biceps, Brachialis, Brachioradialis, Anterior Deltoid)

Secure one end of the band to a sturdy object in front of you at shoulder height. Stand with the shoulder flexed forward to about 90 degrees and grasp the other end of the band. Use the opposite arm placed under the elbow to support and stabilize the working arm *(a)*. Begin with elbow bent to 90 degrees and allow elastic resistance to straighten the elbow *(b)*; quickly return to the starting position. Pause and repeat.

Kick Simulation
(Lower Extremity Muscle Groups, Core Muscles)

Securely attach the ends of the band to a sturdy object behind you at ankle height. Wrap the middle of the band around the foot of the kicking leg. Start with the working leg behind your body with light tension on the band *(a)*. Simulate a kicking motion *(b)*. Slowly return.

Hamstring Plyometric Hip Flexion
(Hamstrings, Gluteus Maximus, Gluteus Medius)

Attach the ends of the band to a secure object in front of you at waist level. Loop the middle of the band around your leg just above your ankle. While maintaining your balance (use support as needed), flex your hip and lift your leg to about 45 degrees and flex your knee to 45 degrees *(a)*. Allow the band to pull your knee into extension while you maintain hip flexion. Quickly pull against the band once your knee is straight *(b)* by flexing your knee back to 45 degrees. Pause and repeat.

Quick Kick
(Core Muscles, Gluteus Medius)

Loop the band around both legs just above the ankles *(a)*. Keep both knees straight as you quickly kick forward and backward with one leg *(b)*. Repeat with the other leg. Kick side-to-side as well. Stand on a foam surface for a greater challenge.

Bat Swing Simulation
(All Muscle Groups)

Secure one end of a long band to a stationary object at shoulder height. Grasp the other end of the band as you would a baseball bat *(a)*. Simulate swinging to a point just beyond normal contact of a ball *(b)*. Slowly return. Repeat.

Tennis Forehand
(All Muscle Groups)

Wrap a long band around your waist and secure the ends of the band to a stationary object. Stand beside the attachment point in the ready position with the dominant arm closest to the attachment *(a)*, then step laterally into an open stance while simulating a forehand swing *(b)*. Slowly return. Repeat.

Tennis Backhand
(Posterior Deltoid, Rotator Cuff, Scapular Stabilizers, Core Muscles)

Secure one end of the band to a sturdy object at shoulder height. Standing beside the attachment with your dominant arm farthest from it, grab the other end as you would a racket. Place the arm in a cocked position for hitting a high one-handed backhand *(a)*. Move the arm forward and outward against the resistance of the band *(b)*. Slowly return. Keep your elbow firm and nearly straight to increase the amount of work done by your shoulder.

Elbow Extension With Shoulder Elevation
(Triceps, Core Muscles)

Stand with the band under your back foot, your shoulder at about 100 degrees, and the elbow bent at 90 degrees *(a)*. Stabilize your serving arm using the other hand, if needed, to ensure that the shoulder stays in serving position. Lean your trunk approximately 30 degrees opposite the attachment point to simulate the serving position, and extend your elbow *(b)*. Slowly return to the starting position and repeat. Note: Avoid placing your shoulder in the overhead position because during service the shoulder is elevated only 90 to 100 degrees because of the side bend of the trunk.

Golf Swing
(Upper Extremity Muscle Groups, Core Muscles)

Secure one end of a long band to a stationary object. Grasp the ends in both hands and stand with your feet about shoulder-width apart. From a golf swing's start position *(a)*, and against the band's resistance, move your arms to the take-back position of the swing *(b)*. Make a golf swing, complete with follow-through, against the band's resistance.

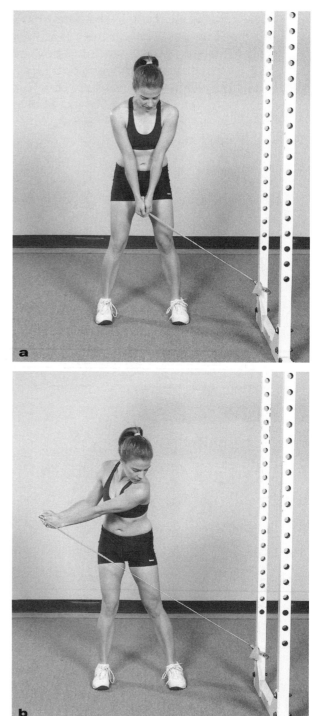

Swim Pull-Through
(Latissimus Dorsi, Triceps, Core Muscles)

Attach the middle of a band to a secure object in front of you at waist height or slightly higher. Start with your knees slightly bent and your trunk bent 90 degrees. Grab one end of the band in each hand with your arms slightly forward and your head in a neutral position *(a)*. Pull your arms back, simulating the pull-through phase of swimming *(b)* and slowly return to starting position.

Jump
(Lower Extremity Muscle Groups, Core Muscles)

Wrap the middle of a long band around your waist and attach the ends of the band to a sturdy object behind you at floor level or have a partner hold the ends. Crouch down and then jump forward *(a)* forcefully enough to elicit light to moderate resistance from the band *(b)*.

Hop Landing
(Quadriceps, Hip Extensors, Gluteus Medius, Core Muscles)

Stand with your knees shoulder-width apart and loop and secure the band around them both with moderate tension. Hop upward *(a)*, keeping the feet shoulder-width apart upon landing *(b)*. Don't let your knees rotate inward on landing.

Jump Down

(Quadriceps, Hip Extensors, Gluteus Medius, Core Muscles)

Standing on a step platform with your knees shoulder-width apart, loop and secure the band around the knees with moderate tension *(a)*. Jump down off the step platform, keeping your feet shoulder-width apart upon landing *(b)*. Don't let your knees rotate inward on landing.

Side Jump
(Lower Extremity Muscle Groups, Core Muscles)

Secure the ends of the band to a stationary object at waist height and stand beside it. Wrap the middle of the band around your waist *(a)* and jump away from attachment point. Land on one leg, and briefly hold that position *(b)*. Slowly return.

Resisted Plyometric Lateral Jump Step
(Quadriceps, Hip Extensors, Gastrocnemius, Core Muscles)

Wrap the band around your waist and secure the ends to a stationary object at waist height. Stand next to the attachment point with a step platform on your opposite side. Place the foot closest to the platform on top of it *(a)*. Jump away from the attachment point and across the platform and back, placing the trailing foot on top with each crossing *(b)*. The band provides resistance during the jump away from the attachment point and assistance during the jump toward the attachment point. Reverse your starting position (turn 180 degrees) and repeat.

Step Jump
(Lower Extremity Muscle Groups)

Wrap the middle of the band around your waist and secure the ends to a stationary object behind you at waist height *(a)*. Place a step platform in front of you and repeatedly jump on and off the step with one foot *(b)*, alternating feet. Keep your body posture erect and well-balanced against the resistance.

Resisted Lateral Shuffle
(Lower Extremity Muscle Groups, Core Muscles)

Stand with the band wrapped around your waist and the ends secured to a stationary object at your side, far enough away not to interfere with running (a). Begin running, or shuffling, sideways against the resistance of the elastic band (b). Switch directions for balanced training.

Lateral Step
(Gluteus Medius, Quadriceps, Gastrocnemius, Core Muscles)

Loop and secure the band around the legs, just above the ankles *(a)*. Quickly step to the side with one leg *(b)*. Repeat, stepping to the opposite side with the other leg.

Side-to-Side Lateral Agility
(Lower Extremity Muscle Groups, Core Muscles)

Secure the ends of the band at waist height to a stationary object beside you *(a)*. Wrap the band around your waist and bound away from the attachment point. Land on one leg and briefly hold that position *(b)*. Slowly return. After several repetitions, change directions and jump to the opposite side, landing on the opposite leg.

Resisted Carioca

(Lower Extremity Muscle Groups, Core Muscles)

Stand with the band around your waist and the ends attached to a stationary object at your side, far enough away not to interfere with running *(a)*. Begin moving sideways, alternating steps in front of and behind your body (carioca steps) against the resistance of the elastic band and attachment *(b)*.

Lateral Bounding
(Lower Extremity Muscle Groups, Core Muscles)

Stand with the band around your waist, the ends secured to a stationary object at your side, far enough away not to interfere with the movements needed to perform lateral bounding. Flex your hips above waist level as you jump laterally and *(a)* return *(b)*.

Fielding Simulation
(All Muscle Groups)

Secure the ends of the band to a stationary object and wrap the band around your waist *(a)*. Take a large, controlled step and bend to simulate fielding a ball *(b)*. Use different directions of resistance. For example, move on a diagonal and go forward and to one side.

Skating Simulation
(Lower Extremity Muscle Groups, Core Muscles)

Loop and secure the band around both lower legs *(a)* and stride forward and diagonally, simulating the stride used during skating *(b)*. Alternate your legs for balance and speed to mimic the skating pattern. Keep looking forward to ensure that the trunk does not bend too much.

PART III

Programming

Functional Fitness Training Programs

The key to the success of any fitness training program is the ability for users to alter or advance the program. This type of flexibility allows users to stay with the program despite temporary or permanent changes in location, schedule, and circumstances. For many people today, including athletes, travel occurs frequently, and working out at a set time and place is not always possible.

Almost all of the exercises presented in this book can be performed in just about any location—a gym, a posh resort hotel, a tennis club, or at home—and at any time. Additionally, the ability of the elastic resistance to provide a consistently reliable resistance for so many types of movements allows for the training and development of the entire body. This chapter offers a series of circuit resistance training programs for overall fitness. The sections are broken into segments that target the upper and lower body as well as the core. One important advantage of elastic resistance and circuit-based program is the ability to shift the focus from session to session. The circuits can be varied to emphasize different parts of the body on different days by, for instance, alternating days for upper and lower body circuits or creating a whole body circuit that encompasses all three main areas—upper body, lower body, and trunk—by selecting key exercises from the lists below and combining them into one repeatable circuit. Finally, these exercises can be performed independently, using safe, solid attachment points for the elastic bands or tubing, or with a partner who can stabilize the elastic material.

Training on the Road

Exercises contained in this chapter are designed to be performed virtually anywhere, making them the perfect choice for individuals who want to stay fit and get a workout while on the road. While all of the exercises use elastic bands, loops, and tubing, some variations of the exercises can be made more challenging by using a pillow, blanket, or rolled towel in lieu of a balance pad or platform that may not be feasible to pack. Because there is often less time to do a workout while traveling, we offer both 15- and 30- minute circuits of exercise training. These include plenty of multiple-joint training exercises, which provide co-contraction of multiple muscle groups and target multiple muscles, creating a very efficient exercise workout. Multiple-joint exercises are very functional and form the key part of any rehabilitation or exercise training program.

Some additional points should be considered when performing fitness training programs on the road or in alternative locations. The exercises in the following programs are designed to be performed in a fairly tight space and use very simple and basic attachment points for the elastic resistance. It is important, however, to be sure the attachment sites for the elastic tubing or bands are secure; hotel furniture and doors may not be as strong and sturdy as objects you use in your regular workout environment. Finally, remember that these programs can be very easily individualized by simply adding a few exercises. You may wish to further emphasize the quadriceps by including exercises from earlier chapters if you have a history of knee injury, for example, or to add a few rotator cuff and scapular exercises if you are a tennis player or golfer.

Circuit Training for Fitness

We chose the circuit training format for the programs in this chapter because of the particular benefits of circuit training. Performing circuit training involves the use of a series of exercises in succession with very short rest periods in order to stress the cardiovascular system. In addition to producing the traditional strength improvements of a training program that uses weights or elastic resistance, performing exercises in a circuit format produce gains in cardiovascular fitness. Therefore, circuit training works the cardiovascular system as it works isolated muscle groups and stresses larger portions of the body through multiple-joint exercises.

There are many variations with circuit training and also many variables that can be manipulated or changed to affect training and, more specifically, the response to training. In general terms, however, performing multiple sets of the exercises in these series and separating them by very short rest periods of only 15 to 20 seconds is recommended. Using a fairly high volume of exercise during the sets (such as 12 to 15 repetitions) will help to promote local muscular endurance, and coupling that high volume with short rest periods allows for a cardiovascular response from the circuit.

In addition to using a repetition-based system of training, the circuit format lends itself very well to time-based training. So, instead of using repetitions to establish the workload, individuals train for a specified period of time. For example, work periods of 15 to 30 seconds, coupled with rest periods ranging from 15 to 30 seconds, are frequently recommended for circuit training. From a physiology standpoint, individuals performing a 30-second work period with only 15 seconds of rest will stress their cardiovascular system more than an individual who works with the elastic resistance for 15 seconds and uses 30 seconds of rest. Changing the work-rest cycle is a common practice in exercise training. For a tennis player, a work-rest cycle of 15 seconds of work followed by 30 seconds of rest mimics the challenge to the muscular system that is encountered when playing tennis. This is an example of the specificity concept, an important factor to consider when determining what amounts of work and rest to use during circuit training.

Another variation within the circuit is the order of exercises. During the circuit format, muscle groups are often exercised in alternating order. For example, an exercise for the biceps might be followed by an exercise for the hamstrings, allowing the first muscle group to rest not only during the short rest period following the first exercise, but also during the performance of the second exercise, which does not involve that muscle group. If, however, the individual wishes to further promote muscular endurance and a greater fatigue response, two or more exercises within a muscle group can be performed back to back, minimizing the rest and further challenging the muscle group or groups in question. Both of these applications are recommended and can be applied to achieve different goals. Simply changing the order of the exercises within a circuit can change the load or demand on the muscle or muscle group in question.

With the types of adjustments we've detailed here, the following exercise circuits are a great way to achieve many fitness goals. Before performing them in a new location, take a moment to be sure that your anchoring objects and methods are sound, secure, and suited for the workout you are about to do.

Upper Body Circuit 15

Suggested Volume: Perform 2 or 3 sets of 12 to 15 repetitions with 15 to 20 seconds of rest between sets and exercises.

Chest Press	page 61
Lat Pull-Down	page 68
Elbow Extension*	page 39
Biceps Curl	page 38
Seated Row	page 66
Shoulder Internal Rotation at 0 degrees	page 35
Shoulder External Rotation at 0 degrees	page 36

* Uses same top anchor as Lat Pull-Down

Upper Body Circuit 30

Suggested Volume: Perform 2 or 3 sets of 12 to 15 repetitions with 15 to 20 seconds of rest between sets and exercises.

* Uses same top anchor as Lat Pull-Down

Lower Body Circuit 15

Suggested Volume: Perform 2 or 3 sets of 12 to 15 repetitions with 15 to 20 seconds of rest between sets and exercises.

Lower Body Circuit 30

Suggested Volume: Perform 2 or 3 sets of 12 to 15 repetitions with 15 to 20 seconds of rest between sets and exercises.

Core Circuit 15

Suggested Volume: Perform 3 sets of 30 seconds with 15 to 20 seconds of rest between sets and exercises.

** Two sets to each side

Core Circuit 30

Suggested Volume: Perform 3 sets of 30 seconds with 15 to 20 seconds of rest between sets and exercises.

** Two sets to each side

Programs for Rotational Sports

This chapter offers exercises for athletes in rotational sports, emphasizing both the extremity and trunk rotation required for many of the rotational sports covered here. Note that both the acceleration of the rotation and the deceleration and control of the rotation are trained in both the base and sport simulation exercises. Improperly overemphasizing the acceleration training is a common training error that can lead to muscular imbalances and ultimately to impaired performance and even injury. Because of its inherent characteristics and ability to work muscles both concentrically and eccentrically (or shortening and lengthening them), ERT allows you to combine the acceleration and deceleration muscular training required for success in rotational sports.

Baseball and Softball

Baseball and softball players perform very repetitive movements, especially during throwing. While the lower body movement patterns are similar to those of many sports, there are some applications of specific movements that can be adapted for these two sports. Injuries from overuse of the shoulder and elbow are particularly prevalent in baseball and softball players, and an emphasis on the development of the muscles in the upper back and shoulder area (rotator cuff and scapular muscles) is extremely important to maintain proper muscle balance and prevent injury. Performing the base exercises for the shoulder and elbow listed here is a key part of an injury prevention program for baseball and softball players. In light of the important role the upper body muscles play in deceleration of the arm during throwing, care should be taken, as with all ERT, to perform exercises that emphasize both the shortening and lengthening phases of the throwing motion.

One specific movement for softball players only would be the underhand throwing simulation for pitchers contained in this chapter. This exercise provides an overload to the muscles that accelerate the arm forward during the windmill-type pitching motion. However, this exercise should be coupled with the rotator cuff base exercises to ensure that a complete training approach is undertaken to protect and optimize function in the throwing arm.

Base Exercises

Sport Simulation Exercises

Batting Simulation
(Trunk Rotators, Gluteals, Quadriceps, Calves)

Secure one end of the band to a stationary object at chest height and wrap the other end around your hand as you grasp the bat. Assume your batting stance and simulate a swing to a point just beyond normal contact with the ball.

Lateral Step Lunge With Glove
(All Muscle Groups)

Secure the ends of the band to a stationary object about waist height and wrap the middle of the band around your waist. Take a large, controlled step away from the attachment bend and reach to simulate fielding a ball. Slowly return to the starting position.

Throwing Simulation With Ball
(All Muscle Groups)

Secure one end of the band to a stationary object at shoulder level and wrap the other end of the band around your throwing hand. Face away from the attachment point and, with a ball in hand, perform a throwing motion, including follow-through, using the resistance from the band to gently overload the muscles used in throwing. Slowly return to the starting position.

Underhand Windmill Simulation
(All Muscle Groups)

With a ball in hand, grasp one end of the band or tubing and secure the other end at waist level to a secure object. Assume a throwing stance with your arm reaching back just below shoulder level. Take a step, using the normal pitching mechanics, and bring the arm forward until it is slightly out in front of the body (just past the normal release point). Slowly return to the starting position.

Tennis

The sport of tennis places unique demands on the body, including multidirectional lower body movements, large, repetitive, and forceful trunk rotation, and repetitive stresses to the rotator cuff and scapular (shoulder blade) musculature. Tennis players, like athletes in throwing sports, often have an imbalance between the muscles in the front of the upper body (the accelerators), and the smaller, often overmatched muscles in the back of the shoulder and shoulder blade region that decelerate and stabilize the shoulder. Therefore, base exercises geared at improving strength and endurance of the rotator cuff and scapular muscles are extremely important parts of a tennis player's training program and are emphasized here. Many of these exercises are performed with the upper arm at a right angle to the body (90 degrees). This position simulates the position the shoulder is placed in during the serve, and these exercises prepare the muscles to perform their functions in the exact position and manner demanded by the sport. Tennis also places significant repetitive stresses on the elbow and wrist; therefore base exercises for strengthening the stabilizing muscles that cross both the elbow and wrist joints are provided. Increased emphasis is given in our program to training the wrist in several directions to ensure that proper strength development for stabilization is achieved. Because tennis players have significantly greater strength in the wrist and forearm muscles from playing tennis, as well as greater grip strength on their dominant side, these exercises are a staple in the prevention programs for wrist and elbow injury in frequent tennis players.

Additionally, the challenges the game presents to the lower body require movement training in all directions. Tennis players average four or five direction changes per point. This requires a lot of lateral movement, as well as acceleration and deceleration; ERT can provide similar loads to help players train for this.

Base and Sport Simulation exercises for this program are listed on page 180.

Base Exercises

Sport Simulation Exercises

Square Stance Forehand Resisted Movement With Racket
(All Muscle Groups)

Wrap the middle of the band around your waist and secure the ends to a stationary object at waist height. Stand in the ready position and step, using a square stance, and simulate a forehand stroke. Slowly return to the starting position.

Rotation With Racket
(Obliques, Core)

Secure one end of the band to an attachment point next to you and grasp the other end of the band in your hands. Grasp the racket with both hands straight out in front and tense your abdominal muscles. Rotate to one side, keeping the elbows extended. Slowly return to the starting position.

Horizontal Abduction (High Backhand) With Racket
(Posterior Deltoid, Rotator Cuff, Scapular Muscles)

Secure one end of the band to a stationary object above shoulder height. With the attachment point behind you, hold the other end of the band and position your arm to simulate a high one-handed backhand. Move your racket arm forward and outward against the resistance of the band, keeping the other arm stationary. Slowly return.

Volleyball

Volleyball has extremely repetitive and demanding lower body lunging and jumping, coupled with specialized upper body movements, including the block, set, spike, and bump. Great control of shoulder rotation is required, especially for the serve and spike, actions that occur with the shoulder in an overhead (90-degree) position. Muscular balance is a key issue for volleyball players, and increased development of the muscles in the upper back and shoulder region helps provide balance and stabilization.

One critical injury often reported in volleyball players is patellar tendonitis. This injury occurs from the repeated jumping movements inherent in volleyball play. Exercises for the prevention and treatment of this injury include quadriceps work focusing on the lengthening, or eccentric, action of the involved muscles. Movements such as the squat and lunge that emphasize the slow descent or lengthening phase are key components of the lower body training program for the volleyball player.

Base Exercises

Sport Simulation Exercises

Serve Simulation
(All Muscle Groups)

Secure one end of the tubing under your foot and grasp the other end of the band in your service hand, with the attachment point behind you. Position yourself so that there is light tension in the band when your arm is in the starting position of your serving motion. Step forward and perform the serve against resistance of the band; then control your return to the starting position.

Overhead Blocking Simulation
(All Muscle Groups)

Place a loop of band around the wrists. With the arms in an overhead position and the hands a few inches apart, move the hands sideways and back and diagonally and back for 15 to 20 seconds. Keep a slight bend in the elbows. Repeat several sets of this exercise.

Monster Walk With Bumping
(All Muscle Groups)

Secure a loop of the band around your ankles. Bump a ball repeatedly and follow it, making small adjustments with the legs to move against the resistance of the band. As a variation, do this drill with a partner and bump the ball to one another.

Golf

Injuries to golfers commonly involve the wrist, hand, and lower back. Exercises to improve stabilization of the wrist joint and lower back are key parts of a training program for golfers. Additionally, very large amounts of trunk rotation are used to generate power in the golf swing, with contributions from the legs and hips playing a key role. Therefore, exercises to improve leg strength and hip power assist the golfer in producing power during the swing. A balanced program for both lower back and abdominal strength is recommended to stabilize the spine, with rotational movements as the predominant movement. Exercises to improve rotator cuff strength are also important because of the role the shoulders play in the golf swing and the important stabilization these muscles provide throughout the golf swing.

In addition to the base exercises, elastic resistance can be very nicely used to provide simulation to several phases of the golf swing. Performing these simulation drills, along with work on balance using foam platforms or stability trainers during the exercise, will add an additional dimension to this training for golfers of all ages and ability levels.

Base Exercises

Sport Simulation Exercises

Golf Swing Acceleration With Club
(All Muscle Groups)

Secure one end of the band to a stationary object at shoulder height and assume the golf stance. Grip both the club and the other end of the band in both hands. From the take-back position, accelerate against the resistance of the band to contact position. Slowly return.

Golf Swing Take-Back With Resistance With Club
(All Muscle Groups)

Secure one end of a long band to a secure object near the floor. Grip both the club and the other end of the band in both hands. Assume the starting position of your swing, and against the resistance of the band, move your arms and the club to the take-back position of your swing. Slowly return to the starting position.

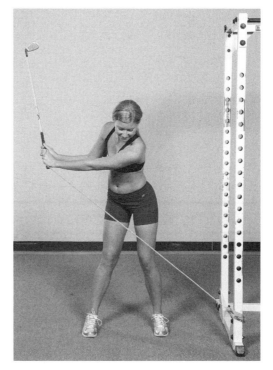

Programs for Strength and Power Sports

Elastic resistance training (ERT) can be a great part of a training program for strength and power sports. Like the other sport-specific programs outlined in this section, our program for athletes in strength and power sports builds a stable base for optimal performance, yet also features specific exercises that train the muscles for the special functions required by their chosen sport. Strength and power sports require a heavy reliance on training the major muscle groups of the body, and ERT lends itself to this approach because it allows athletes to perform exercises at fast, functional velocities in a safe manner.

As a general rule, training for strength and power sports uses a higher resistance base and a lower number of repetitions than the rotational sport-specific training program outlined in the previous chapter, and far fewer repetitions and higher loads than in the specialized programs detailed in the following chapter for endurance sports. With ERT, it is easy to carefully gauge and safely alter the resistance level of the exercises to use a lower repetition base and higher loads to achieve a greater fatigue response.

Football

As a collision sport, football can produce a wide variety of potential injuries ranging from concussions and fractures to injuries of overuse, such as tendonitis and muscle strains. Additionally, the position played can have a dramatic effect on an athlete's training and exercise needs. For example, a quarterback must move in multiple directions, absorb hits, and perform significant rotational movements while enduring the stress of repetitive throwing movements similar to those of a baseball or tennis player. These wide-ranging demands make designing a training program for a football player very challenging.

Two needs among virtually all football players, regardless of position, are multidirectional explosiveness and great upper body strength. Specific exercises, like the rip for the upper body, apply to many positions, as do the lateral and reverse movement overloads, which can be accommodated by elastic resistance at variable intensities. Many of the exercises in our football program work multiple muscle groups, particularly in the lower body, rather than attend to single muscles or groups.

However, football athletes who play certain positions should do some selective isolated muscle group work. A quarterback should include some rotator cuff and scapular exercises in his training program, and players who carry or handle the ball should include some wrist and forearm exercises in their programs.

Base Exercises

Sport Simulation Exercises

Explosion out of 3-Point Stance
(All Muscle Groups)

Start in a 3-point stance with the middle of the band secured around your waist and the ends attached to a stationary object near the floor. Explode out of the stance and take one step forward.

Total-Body Extension
(All Muscle Groups)

Loop the band around the backs of your thighs. Grasp the ends at shoulder height. Bend your hips and knees and assume a crouched starting position. Extend your arms forward and move out of the crouch with the lower body.

Rip Curl
(All Muscle Groups)

Secure one end of the band at waist height to a stationary object behind you and grasp the other end. Step forward with the leg opposite the arm being worked and move the arm up and across the body in a rip-type motion such as a defensive lineman would use. Alternate arms.

Hockey

The challenges hockey places on the human muscular system include the need for explosive power and endurance, as well as the key components of balance and agility. The fact that hockey is played on a hard, slippery surface makes it a unique challenge for the design of both base and sport-specific exercise programs. Injuries in hockey, as in football, vary greatly, a consequence of contact with other players, the ice, and the barriers surrounding the playing area. Upper body injuries, such as shoulder separations, are common, as are groin strains and ligament injuries in the lower body. Because whole-body power and explosive muscular strength are needed, many of the base exercises for hockey, like those for football, emphasize multiple joint movement patterns that encourage strength development in large muscle groups. The sport simulation exercises, however, are very specific and are appropriate only for hockey players.

Hockey players must have balanced strength in the abductor/adductor musculature of the groin and outside hip to minimize and prevent groin injuries. Sport-specific adaptations in strength in the groin must be offset by additional training of the muscles on the outside of the hip to decrease injury risk and optimize performance. Hockey also requires great control over the muscle-lengthening movements used in skating. This means that eccentric, or muscle lengthening, contractions should be emphasized in training, particularly in skating-specific drills and exercises with elastic resistance. The need for players to skate and move in all directions means that elastic resistance training must occur in directions other than simply straight ahead.

All players carry and use a stick during play, making wrist and forearm strength essential for optimal performance and requiring a series of wrist and forearm exercises similar to those needed by a tennis player or golfer.

Base and Sport Simulation exercises for this program are listed on page 194.

Base Exercises

Sport Simulation Exercises

Skating Stride With Stick
(All Leg Muscles)

Loop the band around the lower legs or use an extremity strap to secure tubing to both ankles. Stride forward and diagonally, keeping your feet low and swinging your arms to simulate the stride used during skating.

Resisted Slide and Stride With Stick
(Hip Abductors, Hip Adductors)

Stand on a smooth surface. Loop the band around the lower legs or use an extremity strap to secure ankles. Slide one leg to the side while holding the stick and maintaining an upright posture.

Resisted Slap Shot Take-Back With Stick
(All Muscle Groups)

Secure one end of the band around the end of a hockey stick and the other end to a stationary object. Bring the stick up and away from the floor against the resistance of the band.

Resisted Slap Shot Follow-Through With Stick
(All Muscle Groups)

Secure one end of the band around a hockey stick and the other to a stationary object three to six inches from the floor. Move the stick forward to simulate the contact and end position of a slap shot.

Wrist Shot With Stick
(All Muscle Groups)

Secure one end of the band around a hockey stick and the other to a stationary object at about hip height. Move the stick forward to simulate the contact and end position of a wrist shot.

Skiing

The skier requires exceptional balance, muscular strength, and endurance in the lower body. Upper body extension and propulsion are also needed, indicating the need for exercises that work the triceps and latissimus dorsi. Even with advances and improvements in skis and ski binding technology, injuries to the knee make up the majority (up to 50 percent) of skiing injuries. Strengthening the quadriceps and hip musculature helps to stabilize the knee and reduce the risk of injury. To avoid traumatic injuries from falls, such as shoulder dislocations and upper-body fractures, balance training should be included as well.

Skiers' muscles are worked in complex patterns to both stabilize the joints and allow for specific motions such as turning and other adjustments to optimize their body position. Skiers rely especially on the gluteals, quadriceps, and hamstrings, as well as the adductors (groin) and calf muscles. Action of these muscles allows skiers to maintain proper control of their center of gravity even while using a very limited base of support (the skis). Many of the exercises in this program can be made more challenging to suit advanced skiers, and those who want to become advanced skiers, by placing a balance platform under the feet to add balance control to the exercise. Simply adding the balance platform greatly increases both the challenge of the exercise and the number of stabilizing muscle contractions required during the exercise.

Programs to improve muscle strength and endurance are widely recommended by top coaches and physicians who work with both novices and high level skiers. Using the following modified exercises to strengthen the quadriceps, hamstrings, and gluteals will prepare skiers for the sport's demands, as well as allow the skiers to absorb loads and control their body motion in the many challenging situations they face. Concentration on balance and eccentric components of these exercises is very important.

Base Exercises

Sport Simulation Exercises

Tuck Squat
(Hip Extensors, Quadriceps, Calves)

Assume a tuck position with the middle of a long band wrapped around the lower back. Secure the ends of the band under your feet. Maintain the tuck position while performing a mini-squat.

Balance Squat With Bench
(All Muscle Groups)

Stand on one leg with one end of the band or tubing secured underfoot. Grasp the other end of the band and pull it to waist level. Rest the other leg on a bench behind you. Perform a single-leg squat, bending your knee 45 to 60 degrees. Remain upright and look straight ahead.

Double-Leg Resisted Squat
(Hip Extensors, Quadriceps, Calves)

Stand with the middle of the band secured under your feet. Grasp the ends in both hands and wrap the band up over the top of the shoulders. Perform a partial squat, looking straight ahead and minimizing any forward trunk bend. Slowly return to starting position.

Basketball

The sport of basketball requires very high levels of cardiovascular and muscular fitness. It also is characterized by repeated, multidirectional movements requiring combinations of great strength and power as well as muscular endurance. Upper extremity strength while rebounding is essential; however, strength training for basketball often focuses on lower body and core work to optimize powerful movement and cutting.

One of the most common injuries in basketball is the ankle sprain. Elastic resistance training is an optimal means of strengthening the muscles that protect and stabilize the ankle joint and should be a key part of every basketball player's strength and conditioning program. Because most ankle injuries involve inversion, or rolling inward, of the ankle, exercises to strengthen the muscles on the outside of the ankle using eversion (outward rotation) are important.

Another focus of injury prevention for basketball players is the knee. Extensive research has shown the importance of core and lower body strength and balance in preventing knee injuries. Injuries to the anterior cruciate ligament are common. Preventative conditioning programs emphasizing lower body and core strength as well as balance training are recommended to address and minimize injury risk. The base exercises in this program are geared toward increasing quadriceps, hamstring, and hip abductor strength to stabilize the lower extremities and provide muscular support during landing and cutting actions. Screening basketball players for proper single-leg squatting ability can be used to determine the amount of extra conditioning needed.

Base Exercises

Sport Simulation Exercise

Step-Slide With Basketball
(Core Muscles, Hip Flexors, Hip Abductors, Quadriceps)

Start with the band looped around your ankles. Hold a basketball in both hands in a chest pass position and step laterally, placing more tension in the band. Repeat the lateral step in several directions against the resistance of the band while keeping slight tension in the elastic. If you have a partner or a wall to pass the ball to, repeatedly pass the basketball back and forth to simulate moving and passing movements performed in basketball.

Programs for Endurance Sports

Athletes in endurance sports need to avoid the pitfalls of overuse injury while training sufficiently to prepare for the extended nature of their sport. An exercise program with high loads and few repetitions will not prepare these athletes for their sports and might subject them to unnecessary injury risk. Rather, for them the use of elastic resistance training for high repetition training movements is preferred. Typically, athletes in endurance sports require supplemental exercise training to develop endurance in the muscles that are performing the sport activity and to provide muscular balance by working the underdeveloped and unbalanced muscles that are paired with, and thus work against, the muscles that are performing the sport activity.

Finally, for sports like running and cycling, where development of the main muscles occurs from performance of the sport itself, elastic resistance training provides a training method for stabilizing muscles for injury prevention and overall muscular fitness. An example of this would be the performance of a few upper body exercises in runners to improve posture and overall form, even though upper body exercises will do little to speed their running or decrease their performance times.

Following the exercise programs in this chapter using a low resistance level with the bands or tubing and multiple set-training formats (either 15 to 25 repetitions per set, or time-based sets of 20 to 30 seconds) will help athletes build a strong foundation of muscular endurance and strength.

Soccer

The multidirectional movements and cutting patterns inherent in soccer place great demands on the lower body and core. What is often overlooked is the strength and balance of the supporting leg, which is needed to allow the kicking leg to optimally strike the ball. Large ranges of lower body motion are required, making flexibility of the lower body another key area of focus for soccer players. Muscular strains and tendinitis are common in soccer players. Minimizing the risk of injuries involving the two-joint muscles (in this case, muscles that cross both the hip and knee, including the groin, hamstrings, and quadriceps) requires careful emphasis on not only the concentric (shortening) phase of the training program, but also the eccentric (lengthening) phase. Additionally, ensuring that both the quadriceps and hamstrings are addressed to ensure proper muscle balance is essential.

In addition to the base exercise movements recommended, diagonal patterns and actual kicking motions using elastic resistance should be performed. And although the hands are not used in soccer to advance the ball (except by the goalkeeper), several upper-body resistance exercises are recommended for base strength as well as the use of elastic resistance while performing functional patterns like the two-hand overhead throw. Several sport-specific movements with elastic resistance are also recommended. Hip rotation is particularly important not only for kicking and stabilization but also for the cutting and multidirectional demands of the game.

The intermittent nature of soccer, with long periods of running and very short rest periods, make muscular endurance a top priority. Multiple sets of training with high repetition bases are recommended.

Base Exercises

Sport Simulation Exercises

Hip Abduction With Soccer Ball
(Hip Abductors, Flexors)

Loop and secure a band around your ankles or use an extremity strap. Place a soccer ball just in front and to the side of your starting position. Lunge forward toward the ball with the leg closest to the ball.

Hip Adduction With Soccer Ball
(Core Muscles, Hip Adductors)

Secure both ends of the band to a stationary object a few inches off the floor. Standing beside the point of attachment, loop the band around the ankle of the leg closest to the attachment. With your weight on the other leg, shuffle a soccer ball toward the center of your body.

Diagonal Kick With Soccer Ball
(All Muscle Groups)

Wrap one end of a band around your kicking leg near the ankle, and secure the other end at ankle height to a secure object diagonally behind you. Face away from the attachment point. Begin with your leg lifted behind you and light tension on the band. Simulate the kicking motion. Slowly return.

Controlled Kick Stabilization
(Gluteals, Hamstrings)

Stand on one leg with one end of the band secured to a stationary object at waist height, and the other end wrapped around your non-weight-bearing leg just above the ankle. Maintain a secure, balanced posture. Slowly raise and bend the knee to approximately 90 to 100 degrees against the resistance, then slowly return to the starting position.

Throw-In Simulation and Overhead Pass With Soccer Ball
(Shoulder Extensors, Latissimus Dorsi, Core Muscles, Hip Flexors)

Secure the ends of a band to stationary object at about eye level. Facing away from the attachment point, stand with your arms overhead and grasp the middle of the band and the ball with both hands. Simulate a soccer throw-in pattern, bending slightly forward at hips and trunk.

Swimming

Because of the high repetition base required for fitness or elite performance, swimmers have an extremely high incidence of overuse injury in the shoulder. Research has consistently identified imbalances in the shoulder mechanics of swimmers because of the overdevelopment of the internal rotators (muscles used for propulsion) and the underdevelopment of the muscles in the back of the shoulder and shoulder blade region (rotator cuff and scapular muscles). The repetitive stresses to the rotator cuff and the overhead position of the arm during swimming make the shoulder and rotator cuff particularly vulnerable to fatigue and injury. Resistance exercises that strengthen the muscles responsible for the pull-through phase of swimming help to enhance performance, while those focusing on the rotator cuff and upper back muscles help to promote muscular balance and prevent injury.

Swimmers' compete in four primary strokes but do most of their training in freestyle. Using the same pattern over and over further leads to muscular imbalances. To magnify the muscular imbalances, many swimmers use a dry-land training program that mimics the movement patterns of swimming, training the already powerful propulsive muscles to increase their performance. In addition to all the upper body exercise and trunk stabilization needed in swimming, high levels of muscular activity are needed in the muscles that flex and extend the hip and knee joint for various forms of kicking. The exercises listed in this chapter will help the swimmer minimize some of the muscular imbalances and also strengthen some of the muscles needed for better performance. A very high repetition base and multiple sets are needed to address the endurance demands of this sport.

Base Exercises

Sport Simulation Exercises

Running

While no sport simulation exercises are recommended for running athletes, because running itself works the muscles used for sport performance, elastic resistance training is an excellent way to meet a runner's base training needs. Like swimming and other endurance sports, running requires exceptional muscular endurance for optimal performance and injury prevention. Additionally, running requires a stable pelvis and spine, so supplemental exercises are recommended for runners to improve core stability and hip strength. Since most running is truly straight ahead, runners often benefit from side-to-side exercises to increase strength and stability of the hip, as well as from exercises for the lower back and abdominal musculature.

Elastic resistance training can be used to improve quadriceps and hamstring strength as well as local muscle endurance, using a reasonably low resistance level and high repetition base. Ankle-strengthening exercises are also recommended to prevent ankle sprains and to further support the ankle when running on uneven surfaces, such as trails. Exercises such as the Thera-Band kick and hip abduction are helpful to improve hip stability and stabilize the pelvis. Finally, the use of elastic resistance exercises for the upper back and scapular muscles can benefit the distance runner because poor posture, fatigue, and discomfort in these areas can occur during training and ultra-long-distance events.

Base Exercises

Cycling

At first, one would not think that a cyclist would have much use for elastic resistance training. The sport itself produces fantastic development of the quadriceps and calf muscles from the repetitive movement patterns; however, ERT can develop complementary muscles that can be very helpful to cyclists to round out their training. For example, given the position on the drops, cyclists must endure long periods of time in a trunk-flexed posture, stressing the lower back. Additionally, leaning forward onto the upper arms produces tension in the upper back and trapezius muscles. ERT provides a wonderful training adjunct for the cyclist to work on these muscle groups, helping with riding posture and overall strength development. Because the muscles used in cycling are heavily trained by the sport itself, there are no simulation exercises. However, the base exercises in this program are designed to work the scapular and lower back muscles as well as the hip stabilizers, providing a tremendous stimulus for lower body development.

Given the endurance or repetitive environment that the cyclist performs in, we recommend a multiple-set training format with either 15 to 25 repetitions per set, or time-based sets of 20 to 30 seconds.

Base Exercises

Phil Page, PhD, PT, ATC, CSCS, is a physical therapist, athletic trainer, and certified strength and conditioning specialist. He is the director of the Thera-Band Academy.

Page has worked with the NFL's New Orleans Saints and Seattle Seahawks and athletic teams at Tulane University and LSU. He has lectured internationally on the scientific and clinical use of elastic resistance and developed an educational course on elastic resistance that is being taught in over 30 countries.

He is certified by the National Athletic Trainers' Association (NATA) and was awarded the NATA's Otho Davis Postgraduate Scholarship in 1991. He is the coauthor of two other textbooks, including *The Scientific and Clinical Application of Elastic Resistance.*

Page lives in Baton Rouge, Louisiana, with his wife and four children.

Todd S. Ellenbecker, **DPT**, **MS**, **SCS**, **OCS**, **CSCS**, is the clinic director at Physiotherapy Associates Scottsdale Sports Clinic in Scottsdale, Arizona, and is the director of sports medicine for the ATP World Tour. A licensed physical therapist, he has researched and taught in the field for 18 years.

Ellenbecker is certified by the American Physical Therapy Association (APTA) as both a sports clinical specialist and orthopedic clinical specialist. The APTA also honored him with its Sports Physical Therapy Clinical Teaching Award in 1999. He was chairman of the APTA's Shoulder Special Interest Group and is a manuscript reviewer for the *Journal of Orthopaedic and Sports Physical Therapy* and *American Journal of Sports Medicine.*

Ellenbecker is a member of the American College of Sports Medicine (ACSM) and is a certified strength and conditioning specialist through the National Strength and Conditioning Association (NSCA). In 2003, the NSCA named him the Sports Medicine Professional of the Year. He also serves as chairman of the United States Tennis Association's (USTA) National Sport Science Committee.

Ellenbecker lives in Scottsdale, Arizona, with his wife, Gail.